The New CFOs

The New CFOs

How finance teams and their leaders can revolutionize modern business

Liz Mellon, David C Nagel, Robert Lippert and Nigel Slack

KoganPage

LONDON PHILADELPHIA NEW DELHI

Publisher's note

Every possible effort has been made to ensure that the information contained in this book is accurate at the time of going to press, and the publishers and author cannot accept responsibility for any errors or omissions, however caused. No responsibility for loss or damage occasioned to any person acting, or refraining from action, as a result of the material in this publication can be accepted by the editor, the publisher or the author.

First published in Great Britain and the United States in 2012 by Kogan Page Limited

120 Pentonville Road	1518 Walnut Street, Suite 1100	4737/23 Ansari Road
London N1 9JN	Philadelphia PA 19102	Daryaganj
United Kingdom	USA	New Delhi 110002
www.koganpage.com		India

© Liz Mellon, David C Nagel, Robert Lippert and Nigel Slack, 2012

The right of Liz Mellon, David C Nagel, Robert Lippert and Nigel Slack to be identified as the authors of this work has been asserted by them in accordance with the Copyright, Designs and Patents Act 1988.

ISBN   978 0 7494 6517 9
E-ISBN   978 0 7494 6518 6

British Library Cataloguing-in-Publication Data

A CIP record for this book is available from the British Library.

Library of Congress Cataloging-in-Publication Data

The new CFOs : how financial teams and their leaders can revolutionize modern business / Liz Mellon ... [et al.]. – 1st ed.
      p. cm.
   Includes index.
   ISBN 978-0-7494-6517-9 – ISBN 978-0-7494-6518-6   1. Leadership.   2. Risk management.
3. Finance–Management.   I. Mellon, Elizabeth.
   HD57.7.N487 2012
   658.15–dc23

                                                                                    2011052066

Typeset by Graphicraft Ltd, Hong Kong
Print production managed by Jellyfish
Printed and bound by CPI Group (UK) Ltd, Croydon, CR0 4YY

For our mothers

CONTENTS

ACKNOWLEDGEMENTS

Each of us has had a range of independent interactions with CFOs and finance professionals from a variety of organizations over the years. We started working together as a team in 2008, to create an executive programme to help business unit CFOs and other finance professionals understand their broader and more fundamental role in business today. The team is David C Nagel, who continues to serve as an executive at BP and Rob Lippert, who used to be a CFO and today teaches and consults on finance and strategy. Nigel Slack is a professor of operations at Warwick Business School. Liz Mellon is an Executive Director with Duke Corporate Education and has been teaching leadership for 25 years.

At some point in 2009, Nigel Slack said, 'By integrating finance skills with process and leadership capabilities, we are exploring very new ground here. Should we write a book?' That demonstrates the power of a good question – and here's the book.

We want to thank the CFOs and experts who not only endorsed that we were on the right track, but also let us use their quotes to embellish our own ideas.

Mohit Bhatia, CFO Genpact

Douglas Flint, Chairman and former CFO of HSBC

Bob Gray, CFO of UBM

Bernard Katompa, CEO of Liberty Africa and former CFO

Sir Andrew Likierman, Dean of London Business School and former CFO

Allister Wilson, partner Ernst & Young

We also want to thank the hundreds of CFOs and finance professionals we have met for stimulating conversations that challenged and enhanced our own thinking.

Andrew Grant and Shelley Easton-Leadley are two BP colleagues who offered help and support along the way. Maarten Asser and Simon Carter are two good friends in the extended Duke network whose thinking helped us to extend our own on certain topics. And finally, Mark Dawson, a partner at PricewaterhouseCoopers, who introduced us to Zarin Patel, serving CFO at the BBC. Zarin was kind enough to write the Foreword for our book.

Our editor at Kogan Page, Ian Hallsworth, was incredibly supportive and endlessly helpful. He really did keep us on track in the most genteel way.

It was fun writing this book. The four of us debated and worried at ideas and had several 'eureka' moments along the way as a result. On our writing journey, we overcame everything from concussion to a major wedding (one of our kids, not us) to get this done. We like it. We think it's important. We hope you agree.

FOREWORD

I am delighted to write the Foreword to this book. It's as though the authors were reading my mind when they wrote it. I truly believe that the time has come for CFOs to realize their full leadership potential.

So what makes a great CFO? Not just a good CFO, but a great CFO?

In my experience the answer is quite simple, but also quite complicated. Of course, you need to start with really excellent financial skills and wide experience of putting those skills to work successfully in a broad range of business contexts and climates. Read Chapter 1 and cross check your finance skills against the daunting but accurate list in the Appendix. But these skills are just the foundation. They get you the invitation to the party, but if you are to play a leader's role in making the party swing, then you need to be able to deploy a wide range of non-financial skills too. Otherwise, at the party, you'll be the wallflower with the calculator.

Here are the three additional skills you need to be a great CFO – in no particular order, because you need all three and they inter-relate. First is unquenchable curiosity. When you first take your CFO seat at the board table, you must have a passion not just to understand your own part in the business but also the curiosity to understand – *really* understand – the part played by every other person at that table too. You have to aim to walk in their shoes, to see the business from their point of view, to feel the pressures they feel, to take pride in their successes and understand their failures.

Second, you have to be able to relate to people. By this I don't mean you have to make everyone else on the board your best friend. I mean the ability to build strong and supportive relationships with other board members based on mutual trust. When you have to bring difficult news – and CFOs who don't ever bring difficult news aren't doing their jobs properly – then it will help a lot if you can present that news in the context of tried and trusted relationships.

Sometimes your key audience as CFO will be the whole board. But sometimes your key audience will be just one person – your CEO. It's often said that the CFO is the CEO's personal chief executive and in my experience there is a lot of truth in this. But the relationship goes beyond that. I like the idea that the CFO has to be the CEO's greatest supporter, but also (in private at least) the CEO's greatest critic. Getting that balance right can be tricky! Once again, it comes down to building a strong relationship based on mutual trust.

We work hard to build our finance people's influencing and communication skills. The BBC's core business is story-telling to its audiences (factual and fictional stories), and it is a common currency in the organization. Many of these story-tellers are world class and, as BBC CFO, if you can't turn your numbers into a compelling story you won't engage and excite your audience. This is something we all understand.

Finally, you need strength of character. You need the strength of character to resist groupthink and, when necessary, to say the unsayable. You need to be able to defend your analysis calmly, dispassionately and resolutely, even while the heat rises sharply round the boardroom table. It helps that you come at these problems with the natural scepticism which is part of any auditor's DNA. But at moments like these it will help you even more if, through your unquenchable curiosity and your ability to build strong supportive relationships, you have, over time, achieved the respect and trust of your board. You'll find advice on developing these leadership skills, and on building that critical relationship with your CEO, in Chapter 2.

And, of course, saying the unsayable will always be a lot more palatable if you offer a solution too. And you are much more likely to get that solution right if, through your unquenchable curiosity, you really understand every aspect of your business – the people, the operational processes, the customers and the market. It's easy for a CFO to inhibit change – but it's much more valuable, and satisfying, to *drive* change by using your deep knowledge of the whole business to suggest new ways to look at a problem. In this sense a great CFO has to have much in common with a great general manager. By the way, don't overlook the importance of getting your fundamental operational processes right. This is a neglected part of the CFO's armoury and it's described in full in Chapter 3.

Here's an example from my own experience. In recent years, I worked closely with my colleagues in BBC News to explore and understand the potential efficiency savings possible in newsgathering and news production.

By applying the latest digital technology and new ways of working, we could deliver significant cost savings over five years without impacting quality; quality for which BBC journalism is internationally renowned. It helped, of course, that a decent slice of the money saved was reinvested back into BBC journalism – its one reason why the BBC News website is now such a world beater. Reinvestment of this sort is a great motivator in efficiency programmes. This is part of the CFO's role in moving beyond cost savings and stopping things happening, to adding greater value, which is fully described in Chapter 6.

Is there any difference between the public and the private sectors? I've worked in both, and my experience tells me that at a fundamental level both sectors need the same combination of financial, business and personal skills. However, outside the private sector, like at the BBC, CFOs may also have to help their boards develop innovative ways to measure performance, ways that stimulate improvement in businesses that operate without the discipline or focus of a share price or a traditional bottom line. It's a matter of helping your board identify where measurable value lies in your particular organization. Get this right and the chief financial officer begins to morph into the chief performance officer.

This book is rich with up-to-date stories about how currently serving CFOs are creating value. In the BBC, our shareholders are our audiences, and delivering value to them in return for the licence fee is our 'bottom line'. In recent years we've developed a performance matrix we call RQIV for Reach, Quality, Impact and Value. Reach is a measure of our remit to be universally available to everyone in the United Kingdom (so not just share of the audience but also reaching everyone we can through our content and services). Quality measures are excellence, distinctiveness, originality and innovation and this we measure through audience approval and appreciation ratings, surveys and awards. Impact is a measure of content that is memorable, challenging, engaging and supportive of the BBC's purposes. Value is a measure of our efficiency and effectiveness in delivering public value on behalf of the licence fee payer (such as cost per user hour), including performance against industry benchmarks. The beauty of RQIV is that it enables programmes of high quality but niche interest (an edgy drama on a difficult subject, say, on a minority digital channel) to score as highly as a big audience entertainment show on Saturday night BBC ONE. With RQIV we can compare the value generated by radically different kinds of creative output and make reasonably objective judgements about where the balance of future investment should lie.

And RQIV works with the grain – the culture – of the BBC. Creative programme makers who would chafe at purely financial indicators have learned to respect RQIV, which rates quality as highly as efficiency. And licence fee payers, who, quite rightly, want the highest levels of quality *and* efficiency are reassured by RQIV that achieving measurable value for money is something we take very seriously indeed. As CFOs, we have to work with the business, the culture and our customers in order to be effective.

Finally, let me finish with the subject that goes to the heart of this book – how we build the great CFOs of the future. Great CFOs do not come ready made – you have to build them. So when recruiting finance people, I look for attitude as much as aptitude. I ask myself is this person as passionate about this business as we are? Do they offer forward-looking insight? Do they have strong influencing skills? Are they collaborative in their approach? Do they give sound advice and help others put it into practice? Will they relate to the culture and people in the organization? Do they have the right business skills as well as the right accounting skills? Will they, in their turn, help develop the talent of the future?

In the BBC we rotate finance people every three or four years. About a third move round to gain fresh experience inside the BBC; a third leave the BBC to pursue their careers elsewhere; and this makes room for the final third to be brought in from outside – an injection of fresh thinking and different experience. In this way, we challenge our finance people and provide them with new opportunities to learn and grow.

What all this boils down to is that being a great CFO is about a lot more than just being great with numbers. The numbers are your foundation. But they are just the start of the journey. I'm delighted this book has been written; it unlocks some of the secrets you need to know to make that journey a little easier, exploring ways to translate our expertise into action that delivers value to our organizations. It's a wonderfully clear, engaging, insightful exposition of what it takes to build a great CFO, and filled with practical advice to help CFOs survive and thrive.

Zarin Patel, BBC CFO

Zarin Patel began her career as an accountant with KPMG. Her early clients included the fragrance makers Faberge, the auction house Christie's, and the tractor builders Massey-Ferguson. In 1997 she was seconded to turn around an ailing construction company – now thriving once more. In 1998 Zarin joined the BBC and worked in a wide range of finance functions including leading TV Licensing, which involved her in sales and marketing as well as managing a very large customer service operation. In 2004 she became the BBC's CFO, responsible for a budget of c.£3.5 billion. Zarin judges herself on how much value she creates for an organization and has played a key role in driving change in the BBC to release significant savings and reinvest in the future.

Introduction

Why it matters

Finance is in the news. Like most functions in a business, finance keeps its head down and concentrates on doing a good job. So when it hits the headlines, you can be sure it's for a bad reason. Scandal after scandal has rocked business and we know one thing to be true. In all the corruption, greed and fraud, someone in finance failed to keep up. Someone failed to shine a light on the wrongdoing until it was too late. So now, we've all got trouble.

We've got trouble on two counts. The first is that the bad apples[i] have incited a whole slew of legislation and regulation, making our busy day jobs even busier. The second is that expectations of our role have been elevated to the extent that it is hard to see how we can keep up with the wide range of responsibilities we have today (see the Appendix for a list).

Our book is a call to action for all finance professionals to raise their skills, capabilities and personal impact to a much higher level.

And the world isn't getting any simpler

As the Chinese curse[ii] goes, 'may you live in interesting times'. And we certainly do. As Mervyn King, the Governor of the Bank of England, said in an interview to Sky News on 7 October 2011: 'The situation could be even worse than the Great Depression of the 1930s'.

The track record over the first 11 years of the new millennium speaks for itself. Value creation, when measured by total shareholder return, has essentially been stagnant. Corporate and government reaction to the burst of the dot-com bubble and the collapse of Enron and WorldCom had little to no effect in preventing the speculative excesses in the sub-prime market. When liquidity completely dried up in early 2008, no one – not even Goldman Sachs – knew what was going on. And this is just your day job.

We live in times defined by national and global economic concerns. At the individual level, young people across the globe are finding it challenging to get their first job. Working people are having trouble managing their expenses. Many retired people are more worried about outliving their savings than of dying. Demographically, many nations are on the decline, so that the burden of supporting the pensions of the retired and retiring is growing intolerable. And chronic illness is taking over from disease as the most pernicious threat to people's health.

At the global level, the growing economies in the developing countries, such as China and India, are leveraging the low wages of their workforce to expand output and offer fierce competition to the developed world. They are also putting upward pressure on commodity prices to get the raw materials to feed their industrial machines and growing infrastructure. Other countries face stagnant economic conditions and difficult budget decisions. Is there no let-up?

The new CFO

What does this have to do with being a CFO? Because to be a sound business advisor and a competent creator of value, you have to understand, and have a view about, these broader societal and political changes as well. Value creation is the engine for addressing the economic needs of societies and individuals. It comes from the collective success of countless well-run businesses that bring together raw materials, capital, human productivity, technology and innovation. Businesses are the drivers of good jobs, of supply chains that create more good jobs and of profits. Profits can be reinvested in the business, reward investors and contribute to national priorities through taxation. Good business is a good engine for society, just as bad business fuels fear, corruption and greed. Good business needs good oversight. That's the role of the CFO.

And so your mission as CFO has a higher purpose that transcends the immediate reach of your enterprise and culminates in global macroeconomic impact. Never has financial probity been more important and never has the job of the CFO been so broad or so complex. This book is about how you execute against the job, which has grown bigger than you ever thought it would.

Who this book is for

If you are a CFO, this book should help provide insights not only for daily and longer term application, but also for developing your team. If you are part of the extended finance leadership team, this book can help you see beyond the functional niche within which you may have pursued your career so far. And if you are a budding young professional, with 5 to 10 years of solid experience under your belt, this book can help raise your awareness of an exciting road ahead, should you choose to take it.

The New CFOs is the first book to provide an integrated framework for the success of corporate finance teams in the decade which lies ahead. Have your financial capabilities, leadership style and process capabilities kept up with the new demands? As CFO, it's a bit like being dropped into the driver's seat of a speeding race car – quickly deciding how to read the course, when to make your move, how to block a challenger, when to enter the pit for fuel. But, in your heart, you know that you should be considering more fundamental questions, such as whether your tyres or brakes are any good, whether you have the right engine oil, whether the pit crew is well trained, or indeed whether the car has been properly designed, built and maintained. There's a lot going on.

What this book is

This book is your guide for the journey ahead. Our purpose is to raise awareness of the challenges and opportunities you and your team face and to provide a broad framework to help you to have a bigger and better impact on the value of your business. Our goal is to offer some practical advice to enhance your performance as CFO, based on our extensive research, experience and observation. We are not trying to teach you how to drive, but we are trying to help you take important seconds off your lap time. And maybe even upgrade your vehicle.

And what it isn't

This book doesn't teach you any particular subject matter in Finance. It's not a textbook. We recommend sources that you can consult if you get to one of our topics and realize that you need to learn more. This is a road map of what you need to know, an overview of the extended range of your new responsibilities. It's not enough to surround yourself with experts. If you can't ask the right probing questions, you are creating risk for your organization.

The core proposition

This book is a conversation. It starts by scoping the current challenges and opportunities faced by today's CFO. The modern job description, if you like, of what you have to do. It then looks at the core capabilities that you need to build as a leader and in process management in order to excel – how to do your job. We then tie all three together to look at your biggest challenges – how to manage control, risk and investment. And when we talk about investment, we do mean how you support your business in deciding which investments to pursue and execute. But we also mean how you run finance like a business and make the case for increased investment in the function, to improve your business overall. Lastly, we help you to assess where you are today and how you might target areas for improvement.

In our view, the winners in the next decade will be the CFOs who get the basics right and invest in their own leadership development, so that they can embed the institutional capability to sustain leading performance.

Notes

[i] Bad apples like Tyco and Enron and other stories that you know, some of which we cite in this book.

[ii] Really, no one knows if this is Chinese or not. The closest Chinese proverb actually says: 'It's better to be a dog in a peaceful time than be a man in a chaotic period'.

Becoming a custodian of value

It's tougher than ever

We acknowledged in the Introduction that the role of the CFO has never been more complex. Business today depends on the finance function to fulfill a much wider range of tasks, from operational to strategic, than ever before. This book gives you the opportunity to step back and look at what this very challenging environment means for your job and your function.

In this first chapter, we scope your new job description and contrast it with the traditional CFO job, which is already broad. The coming decade presents you not only with challenges, but also with the opportunity of a lifetime. We believe that you need to think and behave differently as you pursue your important mission – to ensure that the value of your firm is sustained and grows. We cover what this new mindset looks like, as well as how you can develop your extended finance team to think and act in the same way.

We then move on to suggest new ideas that can help you to execute at a much higher level. Chapter 2 covers leadership – some of the ideas may be familiar to you and others novel. But while we 'know' leadership, we often forget to 'do' leadership the right way. So a rehearsal of the most important aspects of leadership in finance is always useful. Chapter 3 introduces process management. Here we grapple with the idea of the finance factory – certainly a new and contentious idea. Be open-minded – we think you will find some new tricks extremely helpful in enabling you to balance all the plates you currently have spinning.

In the three chapters that follow, we spell out in some detail how these new ideas can help you to execute the finance mission – value creation through control, risk management and investment. Finally, we close the book with a self-assessment tool so that you can judge your own current level of performance and what it would take to improve.

As the book cover suggests, it's as if you are in a lift, or an elevator. The first question is, which floor are you on? And the second question is, are you going up or down? Your attitude and approach to value will have an impact on your career and on your firm. Let's turn first to think about the advantages and disadvantages brought to you by your finance background. Which type of CFO are you?

Let's start with the size of the challenge and why it can't be met by the traditional CFO role.

The challenge

There are two types of CFO

Allister Wilson, as a Partner at Ernst & Young, sees a lot of CFOs. It's his job. And he is thoughtful about it[i] – he has co-authored several books on corporate reporting, including *International: Generally Accepted Accounting Practice under International Financial Reporting Standards*. He believes that in the run up to the financial services' crisis of 2008, there were occasions in some banks when the CFO may well have lost control, because of the sheer complexity of transactions that were taking place, market pressure and a lack of adequate governance and accountability. He believes that there is no more important time for the CFO to get back in charge to contribute to the effective functioning of the markets.

> There are two types of CFO in the FTSE: what I call a financial CFO and an operational CFO. The financial CFO focuses primarily on financial control, risk management and reporting. Sometimes the pure financial CFO is not a main board director, is essentially relegated to the role of super-group financial controller and may not be able to supply the independent challenge to the business that is necessary. Conversely, the operational CFO is more like a COO, more deeply embedded in the executive management team and committed to supporting the CEO in the operational running of the business. However, he or she comes from an operations' background and is dependent on a strong financial control and risk management group below for support in these critical areas. Some CFOs try to be both. Such gifted individuals are rarer.

Allister is making the point that most CFOs either have a strong finance or a strong operations background and there are drawbacks with either model. We agree. We argue that this scarcity of CFOs with both an operations and a finance background needs to be fixed. The new CFO needs to understand finance deeply, while being able to challenge the business on its own territory.

CASE STUDY   You're here to keep the score

Larry was lost in thought. He had just completed his first week as the CFO of a fairly good-sized manufacturing enterprise, leaving behind his partnership at a public accounting firm. Larry's rise to CFO had been somewhat unexpected. His new company had originally identified two main internal contenders, who came from two very separate branches of the finance tree – accounting and investments. Larry had learned that these branches retained their distinctive allegiances – the CPAs had cheered on their champion, as had the MBAs.[ii]

But both of the internal champions ended up knocking themselves out of the contest. One undoubtedly had a sharper business intellect, but that sharpness extended to his tongue as well, and the operational executives didn't like working with him. The other candidate was much more likeable, but got caught up in an exposé for supposedly using confidential consultant information in his personal stock trading. And so Larry was recruited into the firm, fast.

What an eye-opening first week it had been. The finance leaders in the business divisions reported to division line executives, and saw their own pathways to advancement being guided by the line, not by the finance function. Larry had met with many of these mid-level finance executives during his first week on the job. Larry knew that much of his success as CFO depended on what the top two layers of his extended finance team did – those in corporate as well as those in the business divisions. Yet he could see their resentment – what knowledge did he have of their businesses? And he could see their eyes glaze over when he talked about integrating all finance professionals – the MBAs and the CPAs – into one worldwide function to cross-pollinate skills, knowledge and experience.

Larry spent the first part of the week with the department heads of accounting, tax and treasury, learning from them about where things stood financially. The external auditors were challenging the chunky goodwill provision the firm had booked when expanding their global reach by acquiring a major foreign competitor. Unwinding this goodwill would depress reported earnings for the next three years. On top of this, the firm was involved in several rancorous tax disputes across the globe. Also worryingly, debt levels were creeping up and the rating agencies were starting to ask a lot of questions about loans to subsidiaries that currently were 'off book'.

And then there was the business itself. Larry had had some inkling of where the firm stood financially, but it wasn't until he had met with the department head of planning that he realized why investors were failing to be impressed. Most of the signposts were pointing in the wrong direction. Production volumes and sales were failing to keep pace with market growth, operating costs were rising faster than inflation and too many new construction projects were behind schedule and over budget.

Today he attended his first meeting of the executive team. He listened patiently as each of the division heads boasted about the successes and breakthroughs they were having. When it was his turn, Larry gave a quick run-through of his concerns about the auditors, the tax authorities and the rating agencies. The Chief Operating Officer gave him a broad grin and quipped, 'That's why we brought you in as the new bean counter!'

However, the smiles disappeared when he began to share his concerns about operating performance and what he perceived to be the firm's weakened financial health relative to industry peers. Finally, the CEO himself broke the awkward silence by putting his arm around Larry to say, 'You take care of the money, and we'll take care of the business.'

With those words still ringing in his ears, Larry packed some weekend reading into his briefcase and headed home.

You have a unique role

Like all the stories in this book, this is a true one. In this case, Larry is not his real name, so we have kept this story anonymous. As CFO, he is facing a significant mismatch between his perception of his role and the role his executive committee colleagues would like him to execute. In a recent study from KPMG International and CFO Research Services,[iii] nearly half of the respondents reported that their departments were playing a greater role in strategic decision-making now than five years ago: 62 per cent said they expected this role to increase still further. Many reported that they were dealing with much more complex organizations than in the past and that an important part of their work was helping senior colleagues understand the implications of this new complexity for the profitability of the company.

So you and your colleagues may not be facing the same push back against taking a strategic advisory role as Larry. But it takes considerable skill to be effective without your colleagues thinking that you are trying to do their job. The chief executive officer works with the Board of Directors and the executive team to agree and execute the main business strategies, to protect the firm's long-term reputation and to present the main external face to the public. The chief operating officer and his or her division heads protect the safe and reliable operational management of the firm's business lines. The functional leads – for human resources, public and government affairs, health and safety and environment, and so on – ensure that their organizations are properly staffed and structured to support business success and, where necessary, to intervene for the greater good of the group to manage risk.

Your job is to manoeuvre among them in support of your CEO to ensure that the firm's value is not undermined, as each of them pursues activities that make sense in their own world, but may not make sense for the enterprise as a whole. This book will guide you in achieving this successfully.

The traditional CFO role

Bernard Katompa, CEO of Liberty Africa, the life insurance company, knows more about this than many. He was Vice President and CFO in a global mining company before he took up the role of CEO in the financial services industry and has seen this relationship from both sides. He says:

> The CFO has to be the brain of the organization and get the other parts of the body to be healthy and grow. The CEO is the head and the head needs a brain in it. As CEO, I listen to my CFO, because I have hired a brain. When I was CFO, I had an open door to my CEO. We talked every day and I alerted him to everything that could have an impact on the business.

Bernard is using this clever analogy to explain how closely, as CFO, you need to work with your CEO. Bob Gray, the CFO of UBM, the global live media and communications company, endorses this idea: 'I don't want to be CEO in my CFO role, but I do want to work with my CEO to push harder on the numbers to get to the real value drivers in the business.' As we will see in Chapter 2, being a strong second to your CEO is critical to your success in value creation. Getting ahead of your CEO can be career limiting.

The traditional CFO role is already broad

There is no question that the fundamental technical demands on you as the CFO are daunting. There are demands for monthly and quarterly financial data; to cut functional costs; to finance the business and manage taxes; to achieve regulatory compliance and respond to inquiry; and to be an advisor and appropriate counterweight to the CEO. The Board of Directors, shareholders, regulators, tax authorities and other stakeholders have greatly increased their requirements of the finance function on the accuracy, level of detail and timeliness of financial reporting. And these increased requirements often come at a time when the resources available to you as CFO are diminishing, with budget constraints due to firms finding it harder to achieve top line growth within struggling economies. Douglas Flint, former CFO at HSBC, the global bank, and now their Chairman, explains it like this:

> Finance is often counter cyclical. You may well need to spend more on accounting and control when you need to cut costs in the business, to ensure you track the benefits and manage risk. Business often needs to cut costs most when revenue is at risk. The CFO has to be able to stand up and argue to build the necessary finance defences so that finances are real and sustainable.

So you need to be strong minded and talented at persuasion, in addition to being good at the day job.

As CFO, you are already in charge of a broad spectrum of financial responsibilities. This includes outsourcing financial data management, quarterly reporting, accounting policy, insurance, tax planning and reporting, treasury activities, provision of management information and managing investor relations, at a minimum. We include a full list of the likely responsibilities of the CFO role in the Appendix (including the expanded tasks that we believe are vital to the CFO role today).

But we face new challenges in finance

CFOs are subject to a whole range of new and challenging external pressures. The traditional responsibilities and activities that fall squarely within the finance function's scope are at the centre of so many of the changes affecting the business world. As the Introduction showed, there are changes in the macro financial environment and in customer preferences; changes in technologies and the opportunities they bring; changes in legislative frameworks, enacted by increasingly panicky governments; and changes in overall culture that shift the emphasis towards social and environmental, in addition to business, performance. It is likely that your firm faces fierce global competition from traditional and emerging market players. Not only have matters become more complex to manage, but the time to manage them has shrunk. There is instant access to information because of the explosion of the internet, mobile communications and fragmentation of the financial media into many more sites competing for attention.

Your role is in transition – or should be

We believe that much of the analysis and response from corporate finance has been piecemeal and reactive. Some even contest that the challenges CFOs face today are only a more intense version of the challenges they have faced throughout their working careers. They argue that there has always been the need to reduce costs, to improve productivity, to respond to regulation and to allocate resources in ways that enhance both the short- and long-term health of the firm. Numerous levers have been pulled along the way – re-engineering, outsourcing, systems' investments, new planning processes and metrics and acquisitions and divestments – and will continue to be needed. We agree that you still need the fundamentals in place. But we also believe that the size of the challenge has escalated.

With all this prior effort, CFOs and their corporate finance teams ought to have developed new capabilities to cope with the ever-increasing complexity of the challenges they face. Yet actual experience seems to dictate otherwise. The emphasis often has been more on fixing the short term and less about creating sustainable value. It's been reactive rather than proactive, an entirely human response given the scope of change you are facing. And yet the writing has been on the wall for some time.[iv] Sustainable value needs the finance fundamentals, like strong controls, alongside identifying and managing risks. But it also needs an enhanced risk mindset and a partnership with the CEO and the executive committee in overseeing the investments required to sustain and create value.

We absolutely agree that you should be working hard to make sure that the basic foundations of your finance shop are in place. If you have some major areas of deficiency, then by all means fix them. But please recognize that much of this is like putting your finger in the proverbial dyke – it buys time, but the solution is not a lasting one. For that, you'll need to move your thinking – and your actions – to a higher level. Let's think about what this looks like.

The new CFO role

Don't settle for a narrow definition of your role

Your job is to make sure value is not only sustained, but that it increases. As CFO you need to decide how you will engage to make sure this happens.

If you make sure the numbers are right, that departmental spending is within budget and that the accounts are published on time, you are certainly covering the basics. But this is not enough. The great CFO is one who does all of this, but then takes the next step, providing strong leadership in elevating the performance of the finance team and for the firm as a whole. You ensure that finance continuously improves its processes, you help the firm achieve its strategic aspirations, you know what is going on in your industry and in the broader business environment generally and you understand how key stakeholders see your firm.

The expanded role of the CFO

So, in addition to the increased pressure on managing the purely financial aspects of the firm, such as the accounts, cash flow and insurance, the CFO and the finance function are increasingly expected to become a strategic partner to the business. An executive from a FTSE 500 company describes it like this:

> Why does a car have brakes? So that it can stop – of course. But mainly, the brakes mean that the car can go faster. It's the same for the CFO. She or he is the brake, not to stop the business, but to enable it to go faster – safely. Not the policing role, the naysayer – but the advisor who helps the firm create sustainable value.

What a great analogy for the CFO's dual role of simultaneously monitoring the business while providing strategic leadership for growth.

So, increasingly, the CFO is being asked to excel at two very distinct roles: first, to provide high-integrity monitoring and measurement of the organization's financial condition and performance; and, second, to act as a trusted advisor and strategic partner to the business to drive sustainable growth and profitability.

On top of all of this, the mergers and acquisitions (M&A) teams of many organizations report through the CFO (even if heavily supported by investment banks). This means that business development and negotiations may also fall within the finance spectrum. There are also other transactions to be managed, such as contracts with service providers and joint venture partners. It is often difficult for the sponsor of a line of business or of a transaction to retain objectivity and the CFO can provide dispassionate advice. As a consequence, the CFO is becoming a critical member of the executive committee, proactively leading and motivating the organization to greater success. This broader role makes you ideally suited to become CEO one day.[v] In both the US and the UK, the most common background for the CEO has been finance. Other regions, like Central and Eastern Europe, are now following suit. But you need to become the new CFO first.

Are you this new CFO?

You have to earn the right to sit at the table and to be heard. Even today, not every FTSE 100 company has a CFO on the executive committee. (The CEO and COO run the company in this model – and the CFO is squarely in 'bean counter' territory.) So step back and ask yourself – are you this new CFO? Are you rising to the challenge of adding the role of strategic advisor to what is already a big job? The self-assessment questionnaire in Chapter 7 can help you to decide. It can help you to identify the next steps in your own development as CFO or in moving towards that role.

But to ensure a smooth succession, you need to start early to develop your team members so that they can grow into this expanded role too.

Develop your people too

More than just you, it is also about your people. They often aren't developed broadly enough. Are you enabling them to broaden their capabilities, so that you can be replaced? Douglas Flint, the Chairman of HSBC, offers us more advice here:

> In my 15 years as CFO, we lost only a handful of people in the function. When I was made Chairman, the succession plan for my former responsibilities was smooth. I had recruited my own successor and jointly the incoming head of risk five years before I moved on. I had a mentor when I was at KPMG who used to (jokingly) say that success comes from working with people who are cleverer than you and then taking credit for everything they do! I really learned from him the importance of giving people responsibility and building their experience up so that one day they are ready to step into your own position.

There are some specific leadership challenges facing you as you try to strengthen your finance organization. One is the relatively narrow career development of most finance professionals, which makes it hard for them to become this broader finance leader. Another is the typically dispersed nature of the extended finance team. It's always harder to build a culture of finance excellence and to develop people when they are spread around the globe. Even if you understand the deeper challenges and requirements facing the finance function today, do your finance team members? You may understand the symbiosis of getting more efficient and effective performance out of your finance activities while helping to improve the business. But do they? And how do you help them to broaden, when often they have been developed along a specialist path?

You tread a narrow path

Finance professionals are typically recruited and developed along one of two major career paths – the CPA, or CA, and the MBA.[vi] The CPA/CA is a professionally recognized certification of financial proficiency, usually grounded in strong accounting skills. CAs and accounting professionals typically are recruited into departments which can immediately put them to work reporting historical information. MBAs on the other hand usually deploy their more generalist skills in helping to manage the forward-looking parts of the business – investment case analysis, strategic planning and treasury activities. Added to the mix are mid-career 'high flyers' from other disciplines like law or engineering, who move into the more generalist finance areas to develop and broaden their careers. Because of their background education, and the extreme breadth of the finance function, it is not unusual for financial professionals to have fairly narrow development paths as they progress through their careers. You need to think about actively managing their career development and your own succession plan in order to cross-pollinate the CAs and the MBAs, to create fully fledged CFOs. This is true for CFOs at the local business unit level, as well as at the higher level of finance function leadership. We need broadly developed finance professionals, who can manage across the full spectrum of finance with the value creation mindset of a leading CFO.

Virtual teams make this more challenging

The second challenge we highlighted above is that many of you are physically separated from your extended finance leadership team. It is one thing to manage the performance and development of people who report directly to you and are physically co-located with you. It is another to lead and develop a team distributed around the world. Your team members need to develop and maintain close relationships with the management teams into which they are deployed and yet they also need to retain their professional independence and allegiance to the finance function. It's a delicate balancing act. Especially for finance professionals who develop deep expertise in the businesses they serve, it is tempting for them to 'go native' and miss the larger requirements of consistently managing group financial affairs. You are going to need to create processes which draw the extended finance team together to maintain a strong professional identity.

The finance professionals who report to the team that reports directly to you are likely to be at an even narrower stage in their development. With backgrounds such as control and accounting, audit, commercial, or IT, they may have limited understanding of the other areas. Frequently, these leaders have succeeded by demonstrating conceptual and communication skills, but may be underdeveloped in core operational skills. They may still be relying on their technical expertise, but have problems dealing with ambiguity and complexity. They may have learned that it is better to convey a sense that everything is under control, rather than to admit personal gaps in knowledge, experience, or service delivery. For this reason, it is important for you to take steps to address their narrow leadership development. Lack of attention to training and developing your own leadership team doesn't just put your succession planning at risk. As we will discuss in Chapter 5, it creates risk for the entire firm. Pay attention to the performance, motivation, development and, perhaps most importantly, the empowerment of senior staff two levels down. You should also expect these people to create the same expectations of their staff, in order to create a sustainable and high performing finance function.

If you don't lead them, how is the function going to bring financial order out of financial chaos?

The new CFO mindset

It's the mindset that matters as much as the finance skills. And this represents the essence of the challenge – because we believe a new mindset is needed today for CFO success. This mindset represents a fundamental break from the past.

As CFO, you must have sufficient acumen across the full spectrum of the finance functions to be able to ask the right questions. Without this capability, your organization may face moral hazard. The questions you ask should address the immediacy of the day, but also be more penetrating and far reaching. Understanding all the key financial disciplines is also the first step in enabling you to develop a new mindset that moves beyond the daily grind and that transcends individual subject matter areas.

This new mindset is about how you view your job as a finance professional. It's about seeing yourself as a true custodian of value. And we believe that value is created and sustained through all of your control, risk management and investment activities working together. The mindset we propose is not an intellectual construct, but a state of awareness. Armed with this mindset, you can have an impact beyond the day-to-day, to shape the functional capability of your finance team and the strategic direction of the firm. Beyond the boundaries of your organization, with this higher level mindset, you can join the ranks of those who are important stewards of the long-term future of their economies.

The mindset of a custodian of value

Value comes from taking care of today's business through robust controls and risk management, while taking care of tomorrow's business by investing wisely. These capabilities are represented in Figure 1.1, where control, risk and investment all have equal roles in creating value. What is important in this definition is that finance is often accused of driving through the rear view mirror. Of course, an important part of the traditional role of finance is in looking backwards, to collate and tally the numbers. But there is also a

FIGURE 1.1 The finance capabilities needed for value creation

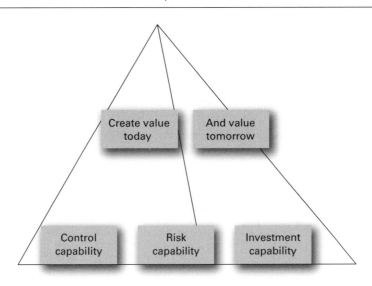

strong role in managing today, through your control and risk activities. And finally, there should also be a component of looking ahead to the future. This is where your role as strategic advisor is played out through investment support and advice.

Once you are clear on what you need to do to create value, the question becomes, how do you execute your role? Being a value custodian is not just about the numerous activities that you undertake as a CFO. As importantly, it is about how you execute. As the song goes 'it's not what you do, it's the way that you do it'.[vii] We believe that the core finance skills shown in Figure 1.1 need to be integrated with leadership and process management skills in order to deliver your mission of value creation. Figure 1.2 demonstrates this.

FIGURE 1.2 Broader skills needed to execute value creation

As we said at the start, in the coming chapters we will describe in detail the leadership and process management capabilities that you need to align with your financial skills in order to be a world class CFO. We will then apply this skill set to show you how to create value across the full spectrum of activities that we believe that the CFO should offer to the enterprise.

Summary ... and looking ahead

In this chapter we have acknowledged the numerous stresses and strains that you face as a CFO, or as an aspiring finance professional. To meet your aspirations at the highest level, we have proposed the importance of you developing proficiency in three core financial building blocks – control, risk and investment. We have stressed that these fundamental capabilities, while vital in helping to sustain and create value for the firm, are insufficient on their own. These financial strengths must be coupled with strong leadership and process management skills as well.

Put simply, finance must respond to a new and challenging set of pressures through three overlapping 'clusters' of hitherto disparate skill sets, which together form a new agenda for finance excellence. These are:

1 Developing core financial skills and a coherent strategy for protecting the value of the business in rapidly changing times.

2 Developing a leadership style that both leads the function and contributes to the shared leadership of the business as a whole.

3 Developing a process-based approach to creating effective and efficient financial services.

We believe that integrating these three arenas – the core financial building blocks, plus leadership and process management – will empower you and your finance team to battle successfully against the numerous external pressures on your organization. You will successfully balance the challenging twin goals of meeting short-term financial goals as well as creating a robust legacy for the firm.

Carpe diem

Without doubt, these are truly exciting times. Finance professionals have the opportunity to contribute in more ways than ever before, while also having the scope for unlimited professional and personal growth. Our belief is that finance is one of the tougher professions, demanding a high and ever-evolving range of skills. We also believe that the rewards are worth it. And remember, every once in a while the CFO becomes CEO.

Leadership – moving beyond position power

In the next chapter, we consider the specific leadership skills that you will need to support you. This is not a summary of general leadership principles. We have worked with and observed CFOs and have concluded that, while generic leadership ideas will no doubt help you, there are specific skills that you will need to deploy. We have identified skills that are especially appropriate to achieving strong finance leadership.

There is plenty of work to keep you busy as a leader – with the day-to-day management of your function, the leadership issues at the top table and your own personal development. Without question, your CEO and executive committee will assess your success or failure as CFO on the big decisions that you take that have a short-term and visible impact on the firm's bottom line and external reputation. These decisions will test your ability to assimilate data, judge risks, recommend a course of action and communicate and implement with clarity.

As we have already said, success will not come from your efforts alone. Your own personal reach is limited. You lead an entire finance organization to support your efforts. Yet, our survey of finance functions indicates that many are in need of reinvigoration in order to become fit for today's challenges. A brilliant captain cannot deliver the championship with an also-ran team – or with a constellation of stars who are unable to connect as a powerful team – or with players who want to focus on the reputation building aspects of the job, while they ignore the fundamentals of their game, like defence.

It's more than position power

We are sure that you have thought about leadership. Our approach in this book is to remind you about some of the leadership skills that you may have overlooked, forgotten or neglected. When considering what it takes to lead, many executives start by pulling out their organization charts. (Step two is often to make an impact within 100 days by moving people around on the same chart.) We accept that the organization chart does describe those people who report to you. But it is also a static description of those over whom you have formal power – to hire, fire, reward and promote. Your standard organization chart won't take you very far when it comes to resolving the inherent contradictions in your role, or in helping you to manage your own behaviour so that you don't erode confidence and support around you. No organization chart can help you to establish credibility with your fellow executives and senior finance leaders. It is of little use when you need to influence and communicate with your finance teams, with the executive team and with important external stakeholders. And we are fairly confident that there isn't a single organization chart anywhere in the world that extends beyond the boundaries of your organization to tell you how to stay connected with the outside world in a way that will improve your performance.

Managing yourself, having a real impact on your organization and connecting externally – these are the core elements of leadership that we think CFOs need for success. Chapter 2 explores these themes in greater detail.

Notes

[i] This work looks at the theory and practice of UK financial reporting. It provides a practical analysis and interpretation of all accounting standards, the related requirements of the Companies Act 1995 and the Stock Exchange, now in its eighth edition.

[ii] Certified Public Accountant, Chartered Accountant and Master of Business Administrating.

[iii] Findings reported at the Chief Financial Officers Conference in Magaliesburg, South Africa, 17–18 August 2011.

[iv] *The Global 50: Perspectives of leading CFOs*, Peter McLean and Carolyn Eadie. As long ago as 2003, SpencerStuart was arguing that the traditionally passive role of the CFO as critic and policeman had changed. They thought the new CFO should be highly influential, serving as a technical expert in finance, accounting and capital structure while also playing a key role in providing operational insights and knowledge. They said that the CFO should be a critical advisor and proactive champion for enterprise excellence, assuming ownership of financial results alongside other top executives.

[v] *From CFO to CEO: Route to the top*, Tibor Gedeon, Karel Pobuda, Andrzej Maciejewski and Robert Nowakowski, SpencerStuart, December 2009.

[vi] Certified Public Accountant, Chartered Accountant and Master of Business Administration.

[vii] 'It Ain't What You Do (It's the Way That You Do It)', is a calypso song written by jazz musicians Melvin 'Sy' Oliver and James 'Trummy' Young. It was first recorded in 1939 by Jimmie Lunceford, Harry James, and Ella Fitzgerald.

Strategic leadership

Seven things you must do well

We know some important fundamentals about leaders and how they are different from managers. You know these too. Leaders make change happen. They think about the future and strive to create it. They create emotional bonds with people to release discretionary effort. People stay or leave organizations because of their influence.[i] They create a climate around themselves – positive or negative. Leadership matters. And let's face it, we all think we do it – don't we? Because we know it, so we must do it, right? But if we are really honest with ourselves, we don't always focus enough on how we show up as a leader – we don't put conscious effort into it. Even though we know how important it is.

As a CFO leader, you already exercise leadership alongside your business leader. What we want to highlight here are seven specific aspects to the CFO leader's role that are critical to your success and to the success of your organization. We believe that you need to be very good at these.

First, you need to be credible as a leader – not just as a finance professional. Being good at crunching the numbers is expected of you and it's the foundation of your credibility. To build on that foundation you need character and the courage to call out situations where your colleagues are finding it hard to face the facts. Play on a broader leadership platform than your functional expertise or your job title.

Second, you need to be outstanding at communicating. You know the numbers inside out, but how do you present information in a compelling way that is easily understood? You need to explain it better, in business language, not in the language of finance. Third, closely aligned with effective communication skills, you need to be good at influencing others. Neither the business, nor the analysts are likely to take your expert advice at face value. They need to be persuaded that you are right. The global financial services' crisis has only exacerbated their caution in accepting that the numbers are right or based on the correct assumptions.

Fourth, you need to develop the capacity to reconcile two apparently opposed ideas and implement them together. Charles Hampden-Turner calls this dilemma reconciliation.[ii] You have been trained in binary thinking – deciding how to allocate expenditure against cost, how to make a decision for or against based on the data. As a more junior finance professional, that was exactly the skill you needed and you have honed it well. As a finance leader, however, you need to develop 'yes, and' thinking – and manage the uncertainty that this creates, for you and for others. F. Scott Fitzgerald expressed it neatly: 'The test of a first-rate intelligence is the ability to hold two opposed ideas in mind at the same time and still retain the ability to function.'

Fifth, you need to be able to learn from failure. Like leadership, that one is easy to say and very hard to execute. We don't like failure from our finance function; it implies the wrong figures, restatement of the accounts and a drop in our share price. But with the best will, and practices, in the world, mistakes still happen. If we cover them up, or assume it to be a 'black swan' event, then we have safeguarded ourselves from the necessity of learning from it. This is dangerous, because it means that it could happen again. You can't engage in continuous improvement without learning from things that have gone wrong, as well as from those that have gone right.

Sixth, avoid derailing. Experts suggest that executives derail – that is, they fail to reach their full potential – more than 50 per cent of the time.[iii] That's an awful lot of executive waste. And we have identified some specific derailers to which you are more prone than the average executive.

Lastly, seventh, you need to network widely, outside your business and outside your industry. We can all get very inward looking, especially in finance, where there are constant demands for more management information and where critical numbers have to be reported on time. But it can make us myopic. The answer to our problem is often already out there – we just need to raise our heads and look for it.

So, seven things to think about. Let's start with your personal credibility as a leader.

CASE STUDY CFO leadership

The air was as tense as it usually was at a meeting with the hedge fund managers. There was a lot of uncertainty and turmoil in the markets and the volatility had everyone's nerves jangling. It had reached the point where it was difficult even to agree on a valuation for companies and Black–Scholes[iv] appeared to have stopped working reliably. Simon was under pressure to come up with answers and the truth was, he didn't have any. He had to decide what to do. He was acutely conscious that his credibility as CFO was on the line. Even if he didn't care about that for himself (and he did), he knew that his every word could be taken down and used in evidence against his company. He had worked there for 15 years and was extremely loyal. Of course, he knew they had a reputation as a company for being a bit stuffy and old-fashioned – but they were still standing, while several significant competitors had found it impossible to withstand the recent downturn. Simon smiled on the outside, while he sighed on the inside. There was only one thing for it. Tell the truth. It was the only way to remember later what you had said:

> Yes we do have plans to grow 10 per cent this year. But honestly, things are difficult right now, so we will do our best, but it is a highly volatile market. As CFO my job is to be as honest and frank with you as possible. We wouldn't have put forward a 10 per cent figure had we not expected to be able to achieve it. But can I guarantee it, in this market? No. We will continue to work as hard as we can and it is certainly not an overly ambitious target. It is not a figure that we have plucked out of thin air, or one that we are working back towards because we have gone public with it. It is what we genuinely believe to be possible. But with the state of the market, I would be foolish to try and sell it to you as a given. Truthfully, I am not sure what is coming next...

And so the meeting went on (and on). It was tough on everyone, looking for answers and clues, when anybody's guess was as good as the next person's. Finally it drew to a close. One fund manager spoke, unexpected words: 'We love it when you come in and speak to us Simon. We get more out of our meetings with you than with anyone else.' Simon was surprised and it showed. 'But I have just spent the last hour telling you that I have no clue as to what is coming next!' he exclaimed. 'Yes', came the response. 'And it's refreshing – because nor do I.'

Being a credible leader

There is no doubt that you are respected as an expert in finance. The higher you climb in your function, the more respected you are. Line managers know that you will respond to their requests for management information, or rebuff the need for more data in a way that makes sense. You have a reputation for bringing the numbers in on time, accurately. You think about risk proactively, not just in a tick-box fashion. You are covering the financial fundamentals well – so why would they want more from you?

Because you are not just a score keeper. You not only sit at the executive committee table, you are also seen as someone whose voice counts. You have a well founded view of the business and your advice is valuable. You have a reputation as a leader that transcends your expertise and your title. Just like Simon in the true, but anonymous story here, executives and analysts want to know what you think because your objective expertise and sound judgement matters.

It would be good to be able to say that every CFO commands attention. In fact, that isn't true. Some never escape the rather pejorative 'bean counter' label. Have you? The twin elements underpinning your broader credibility as a leader are your character and your courage.

Character

In a world where we are going to struggle increasingly with inadequate critical resources – water, investment capital, energy, food and time – the CFO leader has come to be seen as central to decision making. It is so much more than running the numbers and making sure they add up. It is about tough decisions in the face of inadequate resources to go round. It is about ethical decisions that outstrip commercial requirements. It is about foregoing some short-term gains to ensure long-term survival and prosperity.

At the most fundamental level it is about your unquestionable integrity and honesty. If we can't trust the numbers, we lose an important foundation stone in our decision-making. But it is also about more than the numbers. It is about stewardship through some of the rockiest times we have ever seen.

If you can demonstrate the capability to do the job you will be credible. If we know that we can trust you to deliver, you will be reliable. And if you have the humility and openness to listen to others as you decide – if you can let us close enough to understand our needs in addition to your own – you will be influential. Douglas Flint, the Chairman of HSBC, puts it this way:

> Your right to sit at the executive table comes from producing trusted numbers of sound, irrefutable quality – numbers that inform the management team how closely they are tracking their objectives and aspirations. You really have to understand them intimately. Only once you have established the integrity of your technical skill base does your more general insight become valuable. Moving from being an accountant to being a CFO is quite a step and you make the move because you want to be a business advisor. You want to be a business manager with financial expertise. Some CFOs fail because they concentrate too much on the business advisor role, and forget what gave them the right to be at the table. For example, you can't claim that 'the numbers aren't quite ready, I'll need to speak to my people'. You lose credibility – you have to be in command of the financial dashboard that can tell you if something is going wrong.

Douglas is explaining a big transition – from being a finance professional with a good grasp of the business, to being a business manager with an in-depth understanding of finance. He is also warning us not to overbalance on the business advisor side. It's fine for the CEO to ask for numbers to help to take a strategic decision. But not for the CFO. Knowing your numbers as the CFO is the basis of your credibility – your licence to operate. It's important not to walk away from the fundamentals. Your professional training lends you objectivity and cool analysis. Apply it for the good of the enterprise and your stature will be beyond question.

Courage

Part of your credibility also comes from your colleagues knowing that you will call it when you see it. It takes courage and objectivity to have the real conversation, rather than skating politely around it. Your training supports you on at least half of the equation – the 'objective' part. You are expected to be objective and allow the numbers to tell the story. Courage is different. In a way, your training works against you here. You are in a profession that has traditionally seen itself as in service to the business. Especially at more junior levels, you will be familiar with being asked to present the data and then to be largely silent while the business discusses it. It's quite a jump from that advisory role to a role as challenger. This is when being part of a robust finance function, led by someone who is credible with the business, will be important for you, if you are not already that leader. Whatever the business wants from you, a skilled finance leader will expect to see you propose appropriate challenge. You should also expect that of yourself.

Any elephants in here?

Part of your challenge is that you are working alongside colleagues who know exactly how robust, or rickety, are your methods of data collection and aggregation. They know how many are employed in the finance function (the usual view of the number will be 'too many') and the calibre of staff you attract. If you have worked with them over many years, they also have a well formed view of you, as a peer. And peers are the toughest on us, much harder than our direct reports or boss.

With this as the backdrop, you still need to be able to raise, take on, and win, some pretty robust arguments, in order to safeguard the financial probity of your organization.

The hardest will probably be to name and shame a practice, behaviour or attitude that is so deeply ingrained in the way you do business, that no one wants to discuss it. Labelling the elephant in the room, putting the moose on the table – whatever phrase you use to describe telling it like it really is. There will be other difficult conversations that you need to have. You may need to confront the leadership team with a course of action they don't want to take. Perhaps the leadership team is dysfunctional and this needs to be raised, discussed and resolved. You may have to give bad news about the numbers that no one wants to hear. You may have to confront your CEO about an ethical issue, or a decision where his or her lack of knowledge is harmful and potentially dangerous. You may have to confront yourself – perhaps you have let your team down and they need to know.

As Eleanor Roosevelt said, 'You gain strength, courage and confidence by every experience in which you really stop to look fear in the face. Do the thing you think you cannot do.' Raising the issue is the first step in resolving it. But you will also need good communication skills to get your point across.

Good communication skills

There are broadly two arenas where you need outstanding communication skills. One is convincing your colleagues – peers and bosses. And the second is convincing the market.

Sir Andrew Likierman, the Dean of London Business School, is convinced that good communication skills are central to being accepted as a serious member of the senior executive team. He says:

> All professionals – in finance, marketing, human resources or elsewhere – pursue their path because they love the content of what they do. Being part of a team is not high on their priority list. But if the CFO can't communicate clearly, this poses a huge risk to the business. However worthy the analysis, it needs to be comprehensible so that it can alert people to what is really going on. Financial reports that are too dense or boring will be overlooked or dismissed. It's dangerous, because it will stop executives taking decisions fast enough, or stop them from taking the right decisions.

He makes the point that it's not enough to get the numbers out there. They need to tell a good story about what's really going on. Given the fast pace at which business moves, it's not good enough to share data that takes time to analyse. The excellent CFO needs to bring the data to life, to share clear messages with meaning for the busy line executive.

Tell a good story

If you think about the role of storytelling in our lives, it is hugely influential. Parents tell their children parables to teach them about life. *Little Red Riding Hood* tells us not to talk to strangers; *Peter Pan* reminds us that we have to leave childish pursuits behind and accept our role as adults; *Lord Ganesh* explains how a mother's love will overcome any adversity. Anecdotes and stories pass knowledge down the generations in visceral and meaningful ways. We recall them so much better than other methods of communication.[v] Which is why, at your next investor presentation, it's a good idea to tell a story.

Ronald Reagan had his advocates and detractors, but on one aspect of his life we were all agreed. His actor training allowed him to communicate with us in ways that left enduring and vivid images in our minds.[vi] Who can forget his description of the US debt being as high as the Empire State Building? All those noughts (on what today looks like a modest level of debt) were meaningless to most. But the image of dollar bills piled one on top of the other, reaching as high as one of the tallest buildings in New York? That had meaning. So embellish your stories with compelling imagery.[vii]

Get the non-verbals right

Increasingly today, the market wants to hear from the finance professional. The residual but real legacy of the financial crisis is that no one takes the numbers at face value. Analysts, journalists and investors want to hear from the horse's mouth – the one who actually put the numbers together. Financially astute CEOs still have their place and their presence. But you are in demand.

This means that you are in the firing line. As you stand up to speak, they are tracking not just what you say, but how you say it. We know that up to an astonishing 93 per cent of communication is non-verbal.[viii] So people are also paying a lot of attention to how you look and your tone of voice – as well as to the content of your communication. It's hard to believe, isn't it? All that time you spent sweating the system to get accurate numbers out – and they are checking to see if you sound confident in your own numbers and if you look the part of the consummate finance professional.

What this means is that if you have the most accurate numbers in the world and you mumble – you will be less believable than if you have 70 per cent confidence in the numbers but can stand up straight and look your listeners straight in the eye. Ideally, you will have both accurate numbers and an engaging presentation style.

Acting classes

Actors learn status and presence in their classes. In any scene, one character will have more status than others (when an actor gets it wrong, they 'up-stage' someone who is supposed to have greater presence) and, as the story evolves, status levels change to match. They learn to partner appropriate tone with facial expression. (When our tone fails to match our expression or demeanour, we are mistrusted.) They can change the mood of their character from ethos to pathos. Acting classes would be a good investment in your drive to become a more powerful communicator.

Leaders worry, rightly so, about their authenticity. Part of your credibility as a leader is that we know who you are and that you don't try to be someone else. The problem is that many leaders interpret this too literally. It's taken as a licence to be yourself.

Authenticity is not the same as being yourself.[ix] It's about bringing the best of you to any situation. It's about being the best leader you can be. All of us could use a little coaching, whether it's acting or presentation skills' classes, to be the best we can.

Have your elevator speech ready

Sometimes it is simply a case of remembering to communicate. It's not that you don't talk to people – of course you do. But do you have a consistent message? Are you using multiple channels to get this message across? Do you have your 'elevator speech' ready? (Back to the lift analogy. An elevator speech consists of a few pithy messages that you can share with people on a short ride in the lift.)

Bob Gray, the CFO of UBM, started a newsletter to his finance team on the anniversary of joining UBM in July 2010. It sets out his manifesto for the way he wants the finance function to support the business. It is published internally on the wiki and so the whole organization can read it. It doesn't change – but it does get reinforced in conversation with executives, via e-mail messages and at small and large meetings. People in UBM know what finance stands for and what it is trying to achieve for the business.

We've made the point that it's not enough to be on top of the numbers and that you also need to present them in a way that tells a comprehensible and compelling story. But there's more to effective influencing than just telling a good story. Let's now look at our third area of CFO leadership capabilities.

Influencing – not telling

Influencing is about helping someone to see the sense of our point of view and to act upon it. Yet, strangely, one of the best ways to be influential is to show that you are open to influence yourself. If you are too hard and steadfast, you will encourage others to hold their ground also. Show that you are willing to give and take.

The second aspect to good influencing skills is the same as the foundation for all social relationships. You need to listen well (listen to understand) and ask questions (to truly comprehend why the other person holds a different opinion from your own).[x] Yet when we are under pressure or feel stressed (raising the courage to discuss the undiscussable is stressful) is exactly the moment when we listen less well. The higher the stress levels, the more the rational part of the brain shuts down and emotion takes over.[xi] Yet if you can understand why the other person believes what they do – you are then best armed to encourage them to change their opinion by presenting new data and new ideas. You are not pushing them – but pulling them gently towards you.

Asking questions to understand another's viewpoint isn't just about listening to the facts from their side. It's asking questions so that you can understand the assumptions, experiences and biases that sit under their facts. If you reject their facts in favour of your own, you are missing the point. They believe their view of the world for a reason. If you can understand the reason, you are closer to understanding their opinion and to helping them to understand yours. Too often as we look as though we are listening, we are in fact getting ready to speak. The tape running through our head isn't so much 'curious, I wonder why she believes that?' but more often 'nonsense, now what I need to tell him is...' If you can stay focused on the present and be curious about what you are hearing, rather than rehearsing what you plan to say next, you will become more effective at influencing.

Indirect influence

If you work in one of the larger, more complex global organizations, it is unlikely that you will always be in a position to influence straightforwardly a situation that concerns you. It won't be a question of raising the conversation directly, but about working through others and encouraging them to feel the same level of concern as you. One group CFO related this story to us:

> The CEO of one of our strategically important businesses is not good at managing costs. He believes, fundamentally, that you cannot manage costs while you invest to reposition the business. I think he's wrong and I have to consider what level of margin dilution we as a group can tolerate, as his revenues go up, but profitability comes down. I support a new but experienced CFO in the business through back channel conversations. Sometimes I speak directly with the CEO, but his prime relationship is with his CFO. Put bluntly, this CEO needs help, for the sake of the group, so we need to get messages to him in the best way possible for him to be open minded and listening.

We talked earlier about integrity and character. Does this CFO lack integrity? Is he manipulating the situation, rather than being open and courageous? We don't think so. Manipulation is about having hidden goals, often goals to do with personal advancement. That is not the case here. The business CEO knows that the group CFO believes that cost can be managed at the same time as investment. And the group CFO is acting in the best interests of the group as a whole which, as we know, sometimes are not the same as the best interests of a particular business within a group. What the group

CFO is doing is to convey messages to the business CEO in a way that they can be heard. He is being effective in his influencing strategy.

Influencing the CEO – a critical relationship

This is probably the hardest balancing act you will face. You may want, one day, to be a CEO. Our advice is – don't practise by being one with your own CEO. You know the numbers much better than your boss; of course you do, that's your job. You are expected to know your numbers three levels down. But wield that expertise lightly. If you make your CEO look like an idiot, you will not be influential – rather, the opposite.

Douglas Flint, of HSBC, has years of experience here:

> Don't try to look smart so that your CEO has to waste time questioning your motives – whether you are after his or her job. You need to brief your CEO well, so that she or he can answer questions three levels below what they might be expected to have knowledge of. A good CFO makes the CEO look impressive in financial matters. That's when they will reach out to you for advice and rely on you. It's the same in any client service – our best service providers make their clients look good.

Your job is not to show how smart you are by answering on behalf of your CEO. It's to make your CEO more effective through the insights and understanding you provide. This is what creates a star team that the market respects.

Now let's turn to see how you can use these leadership capabilities to tackle the fourth task you must execute well – dilemma resolution.

'Yes, and' decision-making

One of the trickiest aspects of modern leadership is the need for 'yes, and' thinking. What does this mean?

When we consider how leaders thought about strategy as recently as 20 years ago, it was mostly about competitive positioning. This meant analysing the market and then deciding on the place in it that best matched your company's capabilities.[xii] For example, if cost control was your forte, you went for a low price offering. Given that you were better than most others at keeping your costs down, you were able to offer the lowest prices and so capture that market share. Think Wal-Mart. Conversely, if you could differentiate yourself through adding desirable extras to a product or service, you went for the luxury, high price end of the market. Think Luis Vuitton. We all relied on Michael Porter's matrix to position our business for success.

Today the dynamism of the global economy has grown to the extent that adopting and defending a market position no longer guarantees success. In fact, probably the opposite. You could get stuck in a spot that becomes increasingly untenable as the market evolves beyond you. Competitive positions can no longer be reliably defended against the hungry and the agile coming out of the so-called emerging economies.[xiii] The likelihood today is that there is someone nimbler and faster than you out there, who can offer low prices *and* top quality allure. So today, strategic agility has replaced competitive positioning as the key to sustainable success. As an executive, you have to have the ability to read the runes and then to move – fast.

In this new world, what used to be simple choices – high quality *or* low cost – have now become intertwined as 'must haves'. It is no longer an either/or world. It is a 'yes, and' world.

Holding two opposing ideas in your head at the same time is challenging for anyone. And if you have been trained with balance sheets, it can be even harder to develop 'yes, and' thinking. You are more familiar with deciding which side of the balance sheet the money falls – either/or thinking.

And inevitably, this kind of intertwined thinking is not without its problems. It is not straightforward to ally opposing ideas and make them successful and compatible.

It's a dilemma

Gone are the days when you could solve a problem for a single 'answer' – as a leader, you are continually faced with 'and' issues that you have to work through. You know many of these well, for example, profit *and* growth; short-term quarterly results *and* long-term investment. The simple truth is that you have to handle an increasing amount of cognitive complexity.

There are some typical dilemmas that businesses have to face every day – and in addition, you will have some dilemmas that are specific to finance. Let's start with some of the broader dilemmas.

Some common business dilemmas are operating as a global company, while remaining locally relevant; balancing short-term cost efficiencies with long-term growth; benchmarking the competition while drawing ahead of the pack; being low cost and high quality; looking for economies of scale at the same time as economies of scope;[xiv] adopting a common platform while allowing customization; playing the game while changing the game; sticking to the rules while taking advantage of special relationships; co-opetition (collaborating with competitors).

Many of these broader business dilemmas will strike a chord. They certainly provide the backdrop for the specific dilemmas you face in finance today. From talking with CFOs, we find that some of their top dilemmas are cost-cutting today while preserving long-term growth; achieving 100 per cent compliance while keeping costs low; and retaining functional independence while getting close to and supporting the business ('going native'). Do you share these dilemmas?

There are, of course, more specific ones. Bob Gray, the CFO of UBM, shares one that creates tension for him:

> The analysts are under as much pressure as we are. I don't believe in giving Earnings Per Share (EPS) guidance. I think we should provide the analysts with the data they need to make their own projections. Our job is to manage the business, not the share price. But analysts' data are not always up to date and so we need to have meticulous, granular conversations with them to ensure that they can update their projections appropriately. This is enormously time-consuming and it would honestly be easier to give EPS guidance. But it just feels wrong.

Is there some way to resolve the inherent tension between giving behind the scenes direct advice to analysts (arguably doing their job for them) or shouldering the burden of lengthy and time-consuming briefing meetings?

Reconciling the dilemma

Let's walk through the process of dilemma reconciliation.[xv] Just one note of caution. People who choose finance as a career are smart – you have to be, in order to cope with the complexities of the function. But don't bounce into the dilemma reconciliation process as though it were easy. It is deceptively hard. While it is often straightforward to name the two horns of the dilemma, a superficial process of alignment is doomed to fail. This is a rigorous process of thinking through the steps you need to take in order to align and merge two opposing ideas. Let's work through the 'functional independence and going native' dilemma, as this one is truly endemic.

On the one hand, as the steward of financial probity for the business, you need to be fair and be seen to be fair. You need to be able to push back on the line when they suggest stretching the rules too far – the image of a police sergeant comes to mind. Remember all the jokes about Finance being called the business prevention department? If anything, this part of the role has been strengthened since the financial crisis. Business has to get the fundamentals right. Line managers are acutely aware that failure to comply can mean a jail sentence. To maintain your independence, you need strong allegiance to the function and its principles. This allegiance can be reinforced through devices such as keeping the function centralized, so that the finance professionals can advise the business at the same time as holding themselves aloof from it.

At the same time, the finance professional also needs to get close to the business. This is the other horn of this dilemma. Supporting the business in meeting its targets means really knowing your financial stuff. It can also mean being a credible strategist, someone who the line manager wants to consult about strategic moves, whether from a financial or a broader business perspective. And a key piece of being close to the business is having a strong personal relationship with your business partner too. You need to be good colleagues, even friends. This argues for finance being co-located with the business, wherever it is in the world.

Stretch them apart so that you can put them together

These sound – structurally, professionally and even psychologically – very different propositions. That's the plan. To get the ideas together credibly, the first stage is to get them as far apart as possible. Bring out the real differences in the two opposing approaches. If you follow the first horn of this dilemma, you are sitting in HQ in the finance function, saying 'no' a lot. If you follow the second horn, you are out in the country with the business and a golf playing buddy with the local CEO.

The next step is to list the advantages and disadvantages of each approach. The clearer you can be about the detail, the more straightforward the path towards reconciliation. For example, some of the advantages of sitting firmly in the finance function are that you will maintain independence; you will have a clear line of sight into control issues; you will be able to standardize on global processes to be applied in every case; standardization will allow lower cost processes; and you will build strong capability for the finance function. Some disadvantages might be that the business will be disengaged; they may put in place (expensive) shadow processes because you are slow to respond; you will be remote and perhaps not business relevant; and it will be hard to add business value. (We are sure you can think of many more advantages and disadvantages.)

On the other side of the dilemma, being a friend to the business will have the advantages that your incentives are likely to be aligned with the needs of the business; you will be part of a streamlined business delivery team; your advice will be business appropriate; and the business itself will be more agile and able to respond faster. On the downside, you may be building inefficiencies into the business with non-standardized systems; it will be impossible to implement an integrated global strategy on such key aspects as procurement; you will listen less well to the finance agenda; and you may 'go native' to the extent that you fail to offer truly impartial advice. (Again, please add your own ideas to these lists.)

Which way will you spiral?

Next you identify where you are now (which horn do you sit closer to?) and then where you ideally would like to be (what is your goal?). And then, finally, here is where we hit the heart of the intellectual challenge that is dilemma resolution. As you plot your path, which way will you move first? What will be your sequence of moves, chosen from the options listed above? Which obstacles do you anticipate having to overcome? This is where we hit the grey area of decision-making. There won't be one right path that can guarantee success. These are essentially soft issues, where judgement, rather than data, is paramount. And it will be a spiral towards your goal, not a straight line move. You will need patience, because sometimes you will have to take a step backwards in order to move forwards. So whether you choose to put in place a new policy, hire different kinds of people, change your attitude to mobility, or provide finance professionals with different types of training – all these must be sequenced and each will have a different impact. You will only know if you are on the road to success by checking in with the stakeholders affected by the moves – are people buying it or not? And if not, what else must you do?

The key is to know where you are headed – what does reconciliation look like? How will you know when you are there? In this case, the ideal target could be the CFO as trusted business advisor.[xvi] You are still independent, objective and fair and you are also trusted to advise the business well. They might even want advice on which strategy to pursue, or to get support in scoping the strategy from scratch.

Figure 2.1 is a little busy, but it's one we have worked through with a finance team. They chose a sequence that started with moving them back towards their largely neglected role of being independent advisors, while making sure that they didn't look like they were suddenly standing aloof from the business. Can you see how the steps they chose took them first closer to one side of the dilemma and then back towards the other? (Interestingly, not many organizations are decentralizing the finance function in the way that is implied by step 2.[xvii]) And like any other plan, you stop every so often and check that you are still headed where you intended.

FIGURE 2.1 An example of dilemma reconciliation

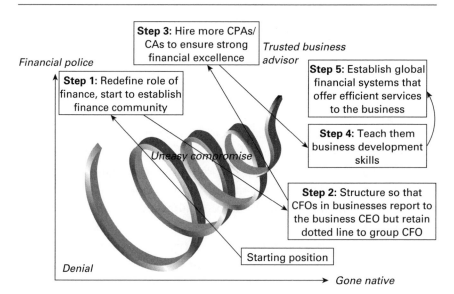

Now let's move on to the next core leadership skill for a finance professional – the ability to learn from failure.

Learn from failure

Again, this is one of those recommendations that gets people nodding their heads sagely. Of course we need to acknowledge and dissect failure to learn from it and to prevent others, in the future, repeating our mistakes. Who wouldn't see the common sense in that?

Yet it is not that simple. Sometimes the organizational culture works against us. And sometimes we, as leaders, fail to set the right tone ourselves. This is not a skill that needs a long list of advice on how to do it. Really it is about seeing the sense in the idea and then having the will, determination and courage to live it.

Reward people who speak out

Allister Wilson, the Partner from Ernst & Young whom we met in Chapter 1, has a strong view about what he calls 'silent running':

> In some finance departments, good control processes are assumed to ensure that mistakes are avoided. That is, everything is deemed to be under control. This is naive thinking. All companies make mistakes, sometimes a big one that requires financial restatement. If silent running is the desired state, and people are rewarded for it, then pretty soon they stop reporting errors and try to cover them up. If the boss sees silent running as success, then inevitably, errors are seen to equate to performance failure. We need leaders who instead see errors as opportunities for performance improvement and engender a corporate culture that encourages transparency and openness. The alternative is a culture of fear that fosters in appropriate behaviours.

Allister is describing a corporate culture that values the wrong thing and drives behaviour in the wrong direction. It would be impossible for a human being to get through life without making a mistake. And every time you mess up, you learn a little bit more about being effective as a mortal. It should be the same with organizations. It is unrealistic to think that everything can be controlled to the point where errors never occur. Instead of making a virtue out of silent running, it would be better to make a virtue out of speaking up when you see something wrong and then working out how to fix it. In public – so that everyone can benefit from your mistake and avoid making the same one. If you reward reporting mistakes – either formally through the appraisal system, or informally through the way you acknowledge individuals as role models – then you will hear about the mistakes rather than being caught unawares by them.

We'll come back to this topic in Chapter 4, where we look at what we can learn from a factory environment in raising and dealing with errors in a routine way.

Have confidence in your people

Douglas Flint thinks it is down to the leadership of the CFO:

> As a leader, you need to both have and demonstrate confidence in your people and be heavily involved in their development. They should never be afraid to put their hands up when things go wrong. And you should be open to bad news – show that you welcome the 'problem', whatever it is.

People are great boss watchers and they will watch what you do, not what you say. Douglas is telling us that it's not enough to tell your staff that they should call it when something goes wrong. How you react when they do so is critical. If you are truly open to the bad news and greet it as a shared problem to be solved – not as a disaster – then you will hear about mistakes. Staff will quickly learn that it is safe to be open about errors and that they will be supported as they move to correct them. What you model as a leader will be the example that they adopt.

We will come back to this topic in some depth in Chapter 5, where we look at risk management. In the meantime, in the next section, we look at your sixth vital leadership skill – staying on the executive track without derailing.

Derailers

What is a derailer? It's a personality trait that we rely on too heavily, or overplay. It's a strength which, through over-use, becomes a weakness. Sometimes it's a strength that was really useful earlier in our career (like attention to detail) that can hold us back in a more senior leadership position (can become a tendency to micro manage). And it throws us off course. We may not lose our job – but we lose our potential to move on to more responsible positions. And the truth is, it's happening more often and it's triggered by stress. As we cited earlier, the majority of executives derail, or fail to reach their potential. We don't want you to be one of them.

As the world in general, and business in particular, becomes more complex, we need to become more agile, in order to respond appropriately. And some of us get stuck and can't. It's a shame, not just on a personal level, where it has a negative and lasting impact on the individual – but also for the organization. It's a time-consuming and expensive waste of human talent.[xviii] And it's avoidable. You don't have to change your personality, but you do have to manage yourself proactively.

Common derailers

Just to reinforce the point, we all have derailers – because we all have personalities. It is part of who we are. It doesn't matter that we have them. The point is that we need to know what they are and manage them so that they don't derail us.

A couple of examples may help. Suppose that you are a natural motivator. You are enthusiastic and energetic. But if you overplay this, you can be seen as emotionally volatile, with unpredictable highs and outbursts. Or imagine that you are a good risk manager. A safe pair of hands. But overplay this and others may instead see you as overcautious and fearful – you fail to balance risk and reward, but default to the risk side every time. Or perhaps you are a thoughtful and somewhat reserved person. We know that the world has an even number of introverts and extroverts, so there is a 50 per cent chance that you are an introvert and naturally somewhat reserved. But if you take this natural characteristic too far, you can come to be seen as aloof and unapproachable – and therefore not effective as a leader. See the full list of derailers set out in Figure 2.2.

CFO flaws

A study by Jeremy Hope[xix] with 362 respondents identified the flaws that were most likely to inhibit a CFO's ability to lead. Indecisive and all talk and no action were top of the list (Excessive caution, in Figure 2.2). Being controlling and micromanaging were third on the list (equivalent to Diligent, in Figure 2.2), followed by being overly deferential (similar to Dutiful, in Figure 2.2), blowing things out of proportion (Colourful, in Figure 2.2) and finally with insensitive, rude and hypersensitive a smaller but significant cluster at the foot of the table (Bold, in Figure 2.2). The first three – indecisive, all talk and no action, and micromanaging were the most significant (everyone identified their top two choices).

Some of this makes intuitive sense. A perception of the CFO as indecisive could come from a tendency to gather and present the data, but fail to offer

FIGURE 2.2 Hogan derailers[1]

Strengths	Overplayed	Become weaknesses
Enthusiastic, motivational	Excitable	Emotionally volatile
Critical thinker	Sceptical	Habitual distrust
Risk manager	Cautious	Excessive caution
Thoughtful, reflective	Reserved	Aloofness
Relaxed	Leisurely	Passive resistance
Confident	Bold	Arrogance
Fun-loving	Mischievous	Mischievousness
Unforgettable	Colourful	Melodrama
Creative	Imaginative	Eccentricity
High expectations	Diligent	Perfectionism
Loyal	Dutiful	Eagerness to please

1–5 Moving away from people; 6–9 Moving against people; 10–11 Moving towards people
[1] Hogan provides one of the best researched instruments on the market.
Look up Hoganassessments.com

judgement based on the data. The flaws Hope has identified may limit your effectiveness as a finance professional, but are they derailers?

CFO derailers

So, the flaws, or potential derailers, derived from Hope's study are Excessive Caution, Arrogance, Melodrama, Perfectionism and Eagerness to please. Are finance professionals more likely than others to derail on these five personality traits? No.

Dr Jeff Foster, who is Director of Research & Development at Hogan Assessments (one of the foremost testing agencies for derailers) shared with us anonymized data on 1,916 finance professionals who have taken their assessment, including 300 finance executives. They did find that the executive group was more likely to be Colourful than the rest of the sample from Finance, which resonates with Hope's 'blowing things out of proportion' above. This indicates that when pushed into a corner, finance executives are more likely than their other Finance colleagues to confront others. Still not a derailer, though.

One thing did surprise Jeff:

> In all cases, and this is a bit surprising, Finance employees are around or slightly below average on the final two scores, Diligent and Dutiful, which represent the third factor of 'moving towards others'. This indicates that they are not likely to respond to stress by overly trying to please others. In general, these trends are statistically significant and interesting.

What does this mean? It means that, as far as Diligent and Dutiful are concerned, finance professionals as a group are statistically less likely to derail on these two than the average business executive. You keep your independence under pressure.

So Hope may have identified some flaws specific to finance that, on average, may hold you back. But Finance professionals don't have special derailing tendencies.

Avoid derailing – manage yourself so you can lead others

There's a problem. The ability to get good quality, honest feedback about your performance is negatively correlated with the rank you reach as an executive. Plainly put, no one wants to give the boss bad news, especially about the loveable flaws that are slowing derailing her or him. It's a strange truth that we watch the boss intently – but rarely comment directly on what we see, even if asked.

So to avoid derailing, we suggest three ideas. First, we recommend that you take a test, like the Hogan one here or similar, to find out what your own derailing tendencies are. One finance executive explained to us that, at home, she never took decisions. At work, however, she had a reputation as one of the most decisive executives on the block. She knew full well that this was a derailer and at work, she managed it. At home, she indulged her personality and let others take the decisions.

Second, work to get good quality feedback. As an astute boss, put in place good quality, informal feedback mechanisms to keep in touch with reality on your performance. It might be a supportive mentor, or a good friend. It's someone who can step inside your office, close the door and tell you the truth, in a caring way. They command your respect and you listen. Third, we know you can't avoid stress, but think about how you are managing your stress levels through exercise, relaxation or whatever works for you. Stress triggers derailers that otherwise we manage to keep under control.

This leads us to the seventh and last aspect of outstanding CFO leadership. How do you keep an active external network alive, when you are so busy with the day job?

Networking to get the broader picture

Finance is a busy function. And it's not busy for the sake of being busy. There is genuinely a lot to do.

It's partly that the job has grown much bigger. Given the global financial crisis, we are keener than ever that you cover the fundamentals of the business well. We want a lot more transparency in the numbers so that they relay an accurate picture of how the business is doing. Having seen Enron fox the markets and bankers trading derivatives that it turned out no one really understood – we want to know what's going on. With regulation increasing and legislation continuously evolving, this is a full-time job even on a national basis. If you throw in the added complexity of working on a multinational, or even a global, basis then the fundamentals get even harder to manage. Cross-border transactions, transfer pricing and currency conversion are a few of the simpler challenges. The bigger the company, the less likely that it has grown purely organically, so now we add the complexity of getting legacy systems from acquired companies to talk to each other (a Heath Robinson[xx] adventure at times). Then the market (analysts, shareholders, commentators) want the reassurance of speaking to you directly and the business wants increasing amounts of strategic advice. You span everything from control to new business development, as we set out in Chapter 1.

Anyway, the point is, the job is hard and the hours are long. What spare time you do have is likely to be devoted to staying healthy and maintaining key relationships, like your family. Networking is not top of your list. And the truth is, it's neglected by most of you.[xxi]

You should get out more

It's not a great idea to be isolated and up to your ears in your own business expertise, in a world where the pressure is on for you to be more of a polymath. At the most fundamental level, you need to know what your finance colleagues are up to in other companies and other industries. You will often gain more strategic insight by networking with colleagues outside your industry. It's a classic problem. If you benchmark yourself against the competition, the danger is that you will swim alongside competitor companies, but fail to gain the insight to pull ahead. And while you are happily swimming together, it is possible that you are collectively missing something – a revolution or a new kind of competition. It's the story of the iPod (invented by Apple, not by Sony or Microsoft) and the twin assaults of generics and genetics on the pharmaceutical industry. All surprises have come from the outside.

More than that, as one CFO wryly remarked: 'If you don't keep up to date with what's going on in the outside world, you are vulnerable to a drive-by benchmarking exercise from HR.' His point seemed to be that it would be better to have an external network from which you can learn fast rather than be subjected to someone else's view of what should be relevant to you.

It's not easy to learn from analogy – for example, learning to apply the principles of retailing in a supermarket to the downstream business in an oil company; or contemplating the similar principles underpinning innovation in order to transfer the process from a government research laboratory to a mining company. But, as we said earlier, you have the cognitive capability to do so, if you work from first principles.

A strategic advisor

More than this, taking a strategic view of the business means understanding some of the really big shifts in the global landscape. We referred to these briefly in the Introduction. Political, economic, societal and technological shifts are playing havoc with 'business as usual'. The days of apartheid in South Africa seem recent,[xxii] yet no longer can a government isolate its people from world events, in the way that the South African government did for decades. Today, the power of social networking can bring down governments.[xxiii] If it can do this to governments, it can surely do this to business too. Being a strategic advisor to the business means understanding these seismic shifts in our global landscape and having an informed view of the potential impact. These are really momentous changes and it is truly hard to make sense of them alone. Informed debate can more successfully deepen and broaden our understanding.

The bottom line is that we can't afford to miss out on networking. Not least because a well thought through point of view on world events can enhance our credibility. And the credibility of your leadership is at the heart of your ability to influence others.

Summary ... and looking ahead

Just how do you earn respect as a CFO leader? The composite parts are set out in this chapter. On top of the core professional tasks of control, risk and investment, you need to be a good communicator and an influential professional, inside and outside your business. You need to be decisive, capable of reconciling apparently disparate ideas and able to learn from mistakes. You need to keep developing, so that you don't over rely on strengths that can derail you as you progress to more senior levels. And the whole package needs to work with people inside and outside your organization. There is a relentless 360 degree view of you out there in the world and you are trying to manage it and polish it so that your organization's reputation is in safe hands with you.

The power of process

In Chapter 3, we turn to how you develop the skills to identify and map your key processes and then improve them through redesign. Effective CFOs recognize that they are service providers for both internal and external customers. They don't just provide the numbers, but they also run an extensive business within a business that provides the numbers. These services include running the back office accounting activities, but also include making accounting policy judgements, managing banking services and relationships, gathering and analysing information about the business, influencing tax policies, auditing the firm for compliance and playing a role in making investment decisions and structuring and closing transactions.

And we suspect that, compared to other areas of your work, you have spent little time studying, and getting your hands dirty in, the world of process management that can help you to improve all these services. In the next chapter, we argue that finance should adopt a process, not a project management, mindset.

Notes

[i] *First, Break All the Rules: What the World's Great Managers Do Differently*, by Marcus Buckingham and Curt Coffman, Simon & Schuster business books, September 1999.

[ii] *Corporate Culture: from Vicious to Virtuous Circles*, by Charles Hampden-Turner, November 1990.

[iii] *The Versatile Leader: Make the Most of Your Strengths without Overdoing it: A Guide to Becoming a Versatile Leader*, by Bob Kaplan and Rob Kaiser, J-B US Non-Franchise Leadership, May 2006.

[iv] Wikipedia explains that Black–Scholes is a mathematical model of a financial market. The model was first articulated by Fischer Black and Myron Scholes in their 1973 paper, *The Pricing of Options and Corporate Liabilities*. They derived the Black–Scholes equation, which governs the price of an option over time. The key idea behind the derivation was to perfectly hedge the option by buying and selling the underlying asset in just the right way and consequently 'eliminate risk'.

[v] *Winning 'Em Over: A new model for managing in the age of persuasion*, by Jay A. Conger, Simon & Schuster, 1998.

[vi] Former US President Ronald Reagan was called 'the Great Communicator'; one of his speech writers claimed that Reagan could read the phone book and make it interesting. Reagan used metaphors with which people can identify. In his first budget message, for example, Reagan described a trillion dollars by comparing it to piling up dollar bills beside the Empire State Building.

[vii] *Made to Stick: why some ideas take hold and others come unstuck*, by Chip & Dan Heath, Arrow Books, 2008.

[viii] *Nonverbal communication*, by A. Mehrabian, Aldine-Atherton, Chicago, Illinois, 1972. Of course, like any good theory, there are ripostes and counter arguments ('Nonverbal dominance in the communication of affect: A myth?', by A. Trimboli and M. Walker, *Journal of Nonverbal Behavior*, 1987, 11(3), 180–190). Try it for yourself. Take a simple sentence like 'the numbers are right' and say it first with a smile and confidence; and then with a frown and a wobble in your voice. Which version is the most convincing?

[ix] *Inside the Leader's Mind: Five Ways to Think Like a Leader*, by Liz Mellon, FT Prentice Hall, 2011.

[x] Chris Argyris, Professor Emeritus at Harvard Business School, is commonly known for seminal work in the area of 'Learning Organizations'. He invented the concept of the ladder of inference – how we take and interpret facts. Because our interpretation will differ from another person, with access to the same or different facts, we will argue based on our different interpretations. Being curious about another's interpretation and where it comes from is the basis for eventual agreement.

xi   *Why Zebras Don't Get Ulcers*, by Robert M Sapolsky, W H Freeman, 1994.

xii *Competitive Strategy: Techniques for Analyzing Industries and Competitors*, by Michael E. Porter, The Free Press, 1980.

xiii BRIC is an acronym that refers to the four countries Brazil, Russia, India and China. It was a term coined by Jim O'Neill of Goldman Sachs in a 2001 paper called *Building Better Global Economic BRICs* and is used as symbol of the shift of economic power away from the developed G7 countries. They are 'so-called' emerging economies in the sense that they are really re-emerging, having been world powers at various times in history. Today we speak more often of the N11 (the next 11 emerging economies). What is generally agreed is that the power house of business is moving from West to East.

xiv Panzar and Willing, 1997, describe economies of scope as increasing product lines (increasing business scope) as a means of cost saving eg spreading marketing costs across a broader product range. Economies of scale are cost savings due to increased production (larger scale) in one product or service line.

xv   Maarten Asser has spent years thinking about the process of dilemma reconciliation and has published on the process. (*The Global M&A Tango*, Fons Trompenaars and Maarten Nijhoff Asser, Infinite Ideas, 2010). He advised us on this section.

xvi *The Trusted Advisor*, David H. Maister et al, Simon & Schuster, 2000, has advice on how to achieve the role.

xvii *How Finance Departments are Changing*, The McKinsey QuarterlyGlobal Survey Results, 2009.

xviii *Why CEOs Fail*, by David L. Dotlich and Peter C. Cairo, Jossey-Bass, 2003.

xix *Reinventing the CFO*, by Jeremy Hope, Harvard Business School Press, 2006.

xx   Heath Robinson was an artist famous for depicting weird and wonderful machines, held together with string and sealing wax – and miraculously functioning.

xxi Ernst & Young, *The DNA of the CFO*, 2010.

xxii In 1990 the then President Frederik Willem de Klerk began negotiations to end apartheid, culminating in multiracial democratic elections in 1994, which were won by the African National Congress under Nelson Mandela.

xxiii The Arab Spring refers to a revolutionary wave of demonstrations and protests in the Arab world. Since 18 December 2010 there have been revolutions in Tunisia and Egypt; a civil war in Libya resulting in the fall of its regime; civil uprisings in Bahrain, Syria and Yemen; major protests in Israel, Algeria, Iraq, Jordan, Morocco, and Oman; and minor protests in Kuwait, Lebanon, Mauritania, Saudi Arabia, Sudan, and Western Sahara.

The finance factory

CASE STUDY Too professional for process?

All the Heads of Finance were there. The meeting room was uncomfortably warm and everyone seemed to be feeling the heat. Nobody more so than James, who found the meeting not just pointless, but profoundly irritating. Sean had been speaking for almost half an hour with hardly any interruptions, pontificating (or so James felt) on his new process initiative. 'We can learn so much from our factories,' Sean was saying, 'They have started to turn this firm around and it's because they went back to basics and asked the simple questions. "What are we trying to do? And what is the best way to do it?" That means a focus on process – on how they can do their work efficiently and effectively.'

It was all too much for James. He burst out, 'Factories are factories and finance is finance. It's ludicrous to compare the two. They make stuff, we are professionals. They deal in tangible products; we have to weigh up sometimes unpredictable and often strategic issues.' What he was thinking was even harsher: 'I didn't spend years qualifying to see my team treated like a sausage factory. We have some of the best brains in the company, we're not process workers.'

A silence followed. It was clear that Sean was making an effort to keep his temper. Eventually he replied. 'Of course no one is denying the obvious differences between what we do and what they do. What I am saying is that, if we learnt from the factory, we could do what we do better. They don't want to make mistakes, we can't tolerate errors either. They need to respond fast to customer requests; we need to get faster at, among other things, quarterly closing. They have to keep costs down, and heaven knows, we are under pressure to do the same. Even if they are different, I don't see your problem with learning from them.' Sean's thoughts were also stronger than his words: 'How do I stop this idiot from derailing the conversation?'

In fact, Sean didn't get the chance to say anything further. It was Sue who intervened. 'Well it's certainly worked for us', she said. 'Most of you know that we set up the new KL operation specifically to do the more routine tasks at lower cost and it's working well so far. In effect, it's a finance factory. We set it up on factory principles, using a process-based approach. Not only is it proving cheaper, it's reducing error rates and it's improving response time.'

James was not daunted, 'OK, for the routine stuff, I'll admit that this process approach may work, but not for the real value-adding decisions where we use our knowledge and experience. Not only is the idea of a process approach not appropriate there, it's downright destructive of value. I bet there's no one here who hasn't been frustrated by some ridiculous, pointless, box-ticking nonsense – try applying for planning permission sometime. Most of this process stuff is just meaningless red tape.' Again, a silence. 'I'd better not tell him that everything can be seen as a process, even his precious "real value-adding" work,' thought Sean','He would really freak at that!'

Who is right?

We found a similar range of opinions in our conversations with finance professionals. Mohit Bhatia is the CFO of Genpact, a spin-off from GE, whose business is in selling financial processes to organizations. Naturally, he is an advocate of a process approach at all levels. He says:

> Finance and accounting is our biggest product – one-third of our revenue comes from services supplied mainly to Fortune 500 companies. These products, which cut across a business life cycle, include compliance, the integrity of financial information, the efficiency of business processes and audit trails. We have a product called Smart Enterprise Processes (SEP), which looks at a company's processes from end to end, across silos, customers, business lines and transactions. We document input metrics that ensure key outcomes are met. We are a process company and understand the science of process.

So who is right? James, who really dislikes the idea of process intruding into his professional skill set? Sue, who sees the idea of process and the finance factory as being appropriate for the routine high volume jobs, or Sean, who sees a process perspective as having something useful to say about even knowledge-based tasks? Or Mohit Bhatia, who makes a living from selling the entire package?

We believe that process is the missing weapon in the finance armoury.

You probably covered process at some point in your finance education and you probably left it right there, a forgotten folder somewhere on your C drive. Its role is possibly limited to debates about cost-cutting, off-shoring and outsourcing – conversations about efficiency gains and labour arbitrage. Frankly, that's a bit old-fashioned.

There are two barriers that stop us taking full benefit of this factory or, if you prefer, process perspective and both are illustrated in this conversation. The first is that we are used to thinking of factories and processes only in the context of the operations function. The second is that when we import the idea of process into our own world, we limit it to routine, high-volume activities. Let's deal with these two points in order.

Factories and efficiencies

It's easy to understand that unless its factories produce products efficiently, quickly and error-free, no business can thrive. Customers become dis-enchanted, revenue suffers, unreliable service incurs extra costs and both long-term reputation and financial performance suffer.

And it's exactly the same for any other part of the business, including finance. Poor service to internal customers, although it may not be as immediately apparent, will eventually have an equally severe effect on the business. A litany of simple processing errors, slow responses, late or unreliable delivery of standard reports, or a general lack of flexibility, distracts internal customers from their prime purpose (which is not coping with your problems). It makes it more difficult for them to serve their own customers – internal or external. And for any company, an inability to report its financial performance, accurately and on time, has real consequences for its market valuation. It also means devoting otherwise productive resources to clearing up the mess.

Conversely of course, a great finance factory will play its part in helping the rest of the enterprise to fulfil its potential. When a finance team develops processes that deliver appropriate, accurate and on-time information reliably and with the flexibility to respond to changes in circumstances, they are helping their colleagues in two ways. First, they are stopping potential errors and disruptions causing problems to other parts of the business. But effective processes do not just prevent bad stuff happening, they also can actively help the business by enhancing positive aspects of service – by making good stuff happen.

Are factories only for the routine?

The second issue is the widely held belief that factories only produce routine and standardized products. Admittedly they are often associated with mass production, but remember that factories also produce some clever products that are sophisticated, nuanced, customized and of extreme value. Communications satellites are made in factories as well as washing machines. In the same way, your finance factory can aspire to produce the highest quality, customized and knowledge-based advice, as well as the more routine services like ensuring that invoices are paid on time.

A process perspective can be applied to a range of tasks; the simple *and* the complex, the straightforward *and* the difficult to define, the routine *and* the rarely encountered.

In this chapter, we will define process and look at its major characteristics, before applying a process perspective to sophisticated advisory services, like law and finance. We will then walk through the five decision points in applying process to finance, from strategic objectives through to building in continuous improvement. We conclude with a short summary of some of the key process improvement tools available today. Throughout, we will focus on choice. It's important for you to choose the right method to map and improve your process, as processes vary widely. Let's turn first to getting clear about the major characteristics we can use to identify and define our processes.

A process perspective

Process may not have the immediate attraction of some other management topics. In the words of one senior finance professional: 'Everyone wants to be a great leader. Who wants to be a great process person?' Yet taking a process perspective is a vital element in the mix that creates a great finance function.

What is process?

So what exactly do we mean by process and why is it important? Formally, a process is 'a set of resources and activities that produce value'.[i] Less formally processes are about 'doing stuff'. If you 'do stuff', you are part of a process.

If you manage people who 'do stuff', you manage processes. So don't think that process is something remote from you. Everyone is part of several processes. Don't try to get away from processes, you can't, because processes are what we do; they are how we accomplish what we want to achieve.

So why do we react against the suggestion that we are all part of a process? The problem is that process is deemed to mean activities that are routine, habitual, repetitive, lacking in creativity, devoid of intelligence, uninspiring and, well, just boring. Worse, adhering to a process implies restriction, constraint, reducing your freedom to act and stopping you doing what you want. And process is just a plain bad idea if it means stopping me exercising my intellect and my freedom. But, as you exercise your intellectual freedom, so the rest of your colleagues exercise theirs, each in their own endearingly different way. And the result is often chaos. Have you ever found yourself chafing against the inefficiencies in your own business because everyone is doing their own thing? One of the reasons that McKinsey is so successful is that they take a strong process approach to their sophisticated advisory work.

There is an interesting analogy with innovation here. The most innovative organizations are those that have strong processes in place, because creative ideas don't get implemented without routines.[ii] One of the reasons there is a dearth of innovation in many organizations is exactly because creative people push back against the idea of being 'controlled'. But it's the only way to move from an idea to an output.

Not all processes are the same

So let's go back to the original definition of process – a set of resources and activities that produce value. And that is exactly what we mean by process, no more and no less. Nothing is necessarily implied about deskilling any-one's job, or always doing things in the same way. No assumptions are being made about always conforming to the same sequence of activities. There is no implicit requirement to specify closely every little activity, nor about rigidly sticking to this specification irrespective of the circumstances. Of course all these things may be a good idea, but not for every process in all circum-stances. That's the point. Not all processes are the same, or, more accurately, all processes should not be the same.

The way we shape and run processes should depend on what we want them to do. What value they should be delivering and what kind of activities are deployed to deliver the value. Taking a process perspective simply means understanding businesses in terms of all their individual processes. The boundaries of each process can be drawn, or redrawn, as appropriate. Sometimes this involves radically reshaping the way processes are organized, for example, to form end-to-end processes that fulfil customer needs.

So they need to be managed differently

Different services produced by the finance factory will have different characteristics, so most finance leaders have a range of different types of process to manage. They are not all the same and here is the important bit – so they should not all be managed in the same way. Process management is as much about the art of discrimination, of distinguishing between different types of process and their needs, as it is about manipulating the details of the process design.

The key distinguishing characteristics – volume and variety

So what are the features that make one process different from another? There are two fundamental characteristics that have a major effect on how processes are managed. They are the volume and variety of the products or services that are produced. And these two are inversely related. Generally, high-volume activities have relatively low variety, while low-volume activities have relatively high levels of variety.

Here is an example from a law firm that has separate teams for each type of service it offers. The managing partner is enthusiastic about how this focused team system allows her to set different strategies for developing each area of business.

CASE STUDY Applying a process perspective to the legal profession

Establishing the various teams has allowed us to discriminate between what each should be aiming for and how they need to improve. For example, look at the contrast between how we manage our Family Law and Litigation practices. In the family law team we help people through the trauma of divorce, separation and break up. Our wealthiest clients value the personal touch that we are able to give them, spending time to understand the complex aspects of their case. All clients are different, and everyone has to be treated as an individual, so we have devised a high-level procedure that still allows plenty of latitude to customize our advice while making sure that we haven't forgotten anything.

By contrast, the Litigation team handles the bulk collections of debt by working closely with the accounts departments of client companies. They have developed a semi-automatic approach to debt collection. The details of each case are sent over by the client and staff input this data into the system and from that point everything progresses through a predefined process. There is a standard diary system for sending letters out at a rate that averages about a thousand a week, queries are answered and eventually debts collected, ultimately through court proceedings if necessary. We know exactly what is required for court dealings and have a pretty good process to make sure all the right documentation is available on the day.

What this firm has discovered is that designing processes that are appropriate for personalized services, where high levels of judgement are needed, is very different from designing processes for more routine activities. High-volume, low-variety processes, like the Litigation example, can exploit economies of scale, can be systematized and maybe automated, all of which can be exploited to reduce transaction costs. In contrast, low-volume high-variety processes, like the Family Law example, have none of these advantages and so can rarely attain very low transaction costs. What they require is enough inbuilt flexibility to cope with the wide variety of activities expected of them. In this case, the processes need to be human skills-centred, defined, but only loosely, with sufficient information to allow an individual to apply discretion in a flexible and adaptable manner. So why bother with a process at all in the second case? Because the law firm can manage, as they say above, to: 'customize our advice while making sure that we haven't forgotten anything'.

Is this starting to make sense from a finance perspective? Are there routine tasks you execute that would benefit from a more systematic approach – like invoice processing? Is there highly skilled advice you offer that requires flexibility of response, at the same time as making sure that you haven't overlooked anything – like an acquisition? Figure 3.1 positions the law firm's services and some typical finance services on this volume-variety spectrum.

FIGURE 3.1 Volume variety spectrum

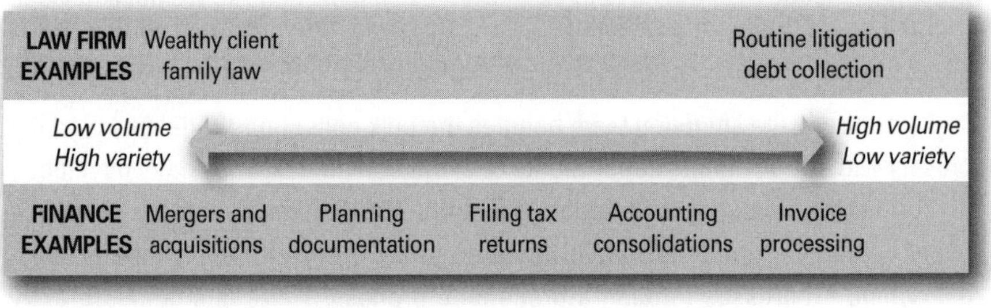

LAW FIRM EXAMPLES	Wealthy client family law				Routine litigation debt collection
Low volume High variety					High volume Low variety
FINANCE EXAMPLES	Mergers and acquisitions	Planning documentation	Filing tax returns	Accounting consolidations	Invoice processing

Designing appropriate processes

Key issues for high-volume, low-variety processes include how best to achieve scale – usually by consolidating each separate activity into a single operation and through standardization. These routine, high-volume and standardized activities are best processed using automated technology, closely defined job specifications with relatively little discretion and tight process control. But of course it would be wildly ineffective to use these kinds of processes to perform activities that are non-standard, knowledge based or diagnostic.

The key issue here is not just that processes differ. It's that you should not use the same approach to designing processes that have different objectives and characteristics. This is really about how you 'do stuff' – any kind of stuff. And in choosing how you do stuff, you are defining your own process. And if you don't like the way you do it, or the requirements change, you can redefine your process so that it works better.

Applying a process perspective to finance

Exactly what are defined as high-, low- or medium-volume activities will vary a little between different organizations. Generally, examples of routine, high-volume financial processes would include invoice processing and payment, cash collection from customers and bank deposits and accounting consolidation (translation of all input data into summary reports by category).

Examples of more knowledge-based, low-volume activities would include accounting policy interpretations, refinancing decisions, mergers and acquisition transactions and developing strategic planning documents. Somewhere in between, medium-volume activities could include preparing monthly operational and management reports, filing statutory reports and tax returns and closing quarterly financial statements. Why don't you think about the finance processes you work with and see if you can place them on your own volume-variety spectrum?

Finance and the process network

Once we understand that all activity can be seen as a process, the next point is that all processes are linked together. Not just your finance processes, but all processes in the business. The inside of any business is a complex and interconnected supply network of processes. Bad service from one process ripples out through the network and eventually affects everything else. So if the numbers from your spreadsheet aren't passed on in a timely way to be consolidated with others, then the delay has a knock-on effect that could eventually prevent you from reporting your results on time – something that would surely affect everything else. Or if your due diligence on a proposed acquisition is delayed, you could miss the opportunity. Process networks are the way that information flows within the business and dictates its operational performance. Every failure to meet internal process performance standards sooner or later will affect overall business performance. And what are the root causes of these problems? It's the way that your processes are designed, operated and continually improved (or not), because processes are what create good and bad service. Some of these processes will be part of the finance function and it's through these processes that the finance factory makes its contribution.

There are two responsibilities

This implies two sets of process responsibilities. The first is to make sure that your processes give great service by performing their activities efficiently and effectively. You do this by continuously improving the processes for which you are responsible, thus giving better service to your customers. But in addition you will have your own unique financial perspective on how all the other processes in the business operate. We all have a responsibility to exploit our particular expertise for the benefit of the business. In other words, the second responsibility is to leverage our expertise in working out ways of helping the rest of the business to improve their own processes. This is especially true where their inefficiencies may have a knock-on effect on the efficiency of our finance services.

So why is an understanding of process management and process behaviour important for developing these two responsibilities? Well, for the first responsibility of making your own processes better, it's obvious. Without a thorough understanding of how processes behave generally and what tools have been developed to improve them, how can you be effective at improving your own processes? You literally won't know what you are doing. For the second responsibility, helping the rest of the business to improve their processes, a good knowledge of process behaviour is also vital. The expertise of any function is many times more effective when it is applied appropriately in context. In other words, expert knowledge should be delivered in a way that takes into account the effect it will have on your internal customers' processes. And how can that happen without an understanding of processes generally?

Anyone can use a hammer, saw and chisel to hack away at a piece of wood. But a craftsperson understands not only how to use the tools effectively, but also knows how the material behaves when it's worked upon. So let's walk through the five decision points in applying process to finance, from strategic objectives through to building in continuous improvement, so that you can become a master at your craft.

Achieving a great finance factory

To summarize where we are, all types of value-adding activity can be viewed as processes and you are part of, or manage, a finance factory that is made up of a network of processes. But these processes are not the same as each other. They differ in terms of their volume and variety characteristics and so they should be designed, managed and developed differently over time. Furthermore, as a finance executive, you are committing to two critical responsibilities. The first is improving the processes that create the financial services you deliver to the rest of the organization and the second is taking some degree of responsibility for helping to improve other processes in the organization.

How?

In this chapter we are making the case for process management at the heart of running an effective finance factory. Generally, the strategic importance of process management is being recognized[iii] irrespective of whether these processes are in operations, finance, marketing, human resources, or any other part of the organization. While there is not sufficient room to deal with every process management issue, if you want to make certain that your processes are making a real contribution, consider the key process related decisions shown in Figure 3.2 and then described in the rest of the chapter.

FIGURE 3.2 Key issues in developing the finance factory

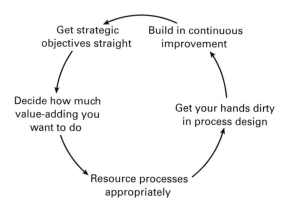

Step 1: Get strategic objectives straight

This should be the starting point for all process development, including finance processes. Paying attention to processes has proven short-term and long-term impact. Just look at the impact that process management can have on cost, service, risk, investment and capabilities, as follows:

1 *Cost:* well-designed and appropriately resourced processes should not waste effort, time, or capacity.

2 *Service:* well-designed processes should understand what their internal or external customers require and build in to their operating objectives agreed standards for what they will do (service specification); what they won't do (error-free); when they will do it (the timing of service delivery); the range of things they will do (service flexibility); and how much they will improve their services (development).

3 *Risk:* well-designed processes should build in mechanisms to identify potential failure points, prevent failures taking place, mitigate their effects and recover from any failures that do occur. (We pick this up again in Chapter 5.)

4 *Investment:* process designers rarely have a blank cheque. The effective use of the capital resources invested in a process can transform it from good but expensive, to just good.

5 *Capabilities:* well-designed processes should be able to learn from their experiences and build this learning into the capabilities that help the process to introduce novel, better or more effective services, processes, methods or ideas.

So these are the generic objectives for all processes. Can you see how they apply to every activity in the finance function? All CFOs would like their activities to be cheaper, better, less risky, have a better return and be more innovative.

Of course, you can't be equally good at all these objectives at once. You have to decide which are the most important and prioritize them. And the relative priority of these objectives will differ greatly depending on what you are trying to do. That is, pick the objectives that link mostly closely to your strategy. For example, if you run a finance business service centre for a global company, cost issues are likely to dominate. If you are in the control function of an investment bank, risk objectives will dictate much of your process. If your organization is operating in a fast-changing market, it will want its finance function to be as flexible as the rest of the organization. And so on. The key point is that there should be a clear, logical connection between the performance objectives set for any finance process and the strategic priorities of the business as a whole.

Please don't dismiss this point as being too obvious. There are plenty of finance functions that really do attempt to take the same approach to designing their processes irrespective of their strategic contribution. That is, they do stuff right, without connecting it to how finance helps the organization as a whole to get its stuff right. But polishing what you do in the abstract makes no sense as a service provider.

One finance professional we know runs an off-shored finance function in Hyderabad, India. Through close attention to strategic objectives, he has transformed what started out as an off-shored service designed to save money, into a centre of excellence that guides best practice. This is what he says about it:

> Getting your overall strategic objectives straight is an absolute prerequisite. Unless you are clear in what you want to do, you can't make any progress

in achieving your goals. The main questions are what are our capabilities? What are we trying to achieve? What is the problem that we are trying to solve? Once you are clear on these questions you can move on to identifying the core activities that will be necessary to achieve the objectives. And once you have done this – that is when you can define the journey for each part of the firm.

This executive has moved well beyond his original remit of simple cost savings. Through paying attention to the strategic objectives of the organization, and building capabilities to deliver the finance services to meet them, he now leads global best practice. This is good for the finance function and good for the business as a whole.

Step 2: Decide how much value-adding you want to do

Once the strategic objectives of each process in the finance factory have been clearly and logically linked to its performance objectives, the first major resourcing decision is what you want to do and what you want someone else to do. One of the trends over the last few years has been to outsource processing, either to specialist internal centres, often called shared services, or to external service suppliers. It's not just finance, operations in all types of business have been moving in the same direction.

Why is this? It is because there are many activities that external suppliers can do better or cheaper or both. So if whole businesses bow to this logic, why not the finance function? It too wants to reduce its costs, make the most of enhanced technology and increase the quality and flexibility of its services. On the people side, it wants access to superior expertise, to avoid short-term labour shortages and to take the opportunity to shift existing staff to higher value work. All of these benefits are, at least theoretically, possible through outsourcing.

Nevertheless it is the potential for cost savings that has dominated outsourcing discussions for years. Back in the 1980s, Ford realized that it made little sense to use hundreds of individual accounting centres across their global networks to perform essentially the same routine financial activities. By using standardized processes and integrated information technology, they cut the number of centres down from hundreds to a handful, with dramatic cost savings. Other early adopters also found that productivity in the shared service processing centres typically increased from each person processing about 10,000 invoices per year, to 25,000 or even 50,000 per year. For example, Intel calculated that it had cut the cost of processing one invoice from $8 to less than $1.[iv] This is why the main driver of out-/in-sourcing has always been cost savings – the savings have been impressive. One business process advisory group[v] estimated that shared services had halved the median cost of the finance function across the business as a whole from 2.5 per cent of total revenue to 1.25 per cent.

Can it bring advantages other than cost savings, however impressive these are? 'People talk a lot about looking beyond cost cutting when it comes to outsourcing', says Jim Madden, CEO of Exult, the California-based specialist outsourcing company. And he continues: 'I don't believe any company will sign up for this [outsourcing] without cost reduction being part of it, but for [our] clients, such as Bank of America, it is never just about saving money'.[vi] Jim challenges us to think about advantages in addition to cost-cutting, when we take outsourcing decisions. The following section considers some of the other angles we might want to take into account as we decide whether to outsource, or not.

To outsource or not to outsource?

There are several other factors, often less tangible, that also should be taken into account before committing to an outsourcing strategy. If an activity has long-term strategic importance, it is unlikely to be a candidate for outsourcing. For example, who would outsource company level financial forecasting? It's strategically sensitive and exposes the firm to the risk of restatements. Nor would a company usually outsource an activity where it had specialized skills or knowledge. If a mining company has built up specialized knowledge in the valuation of potential exploration assets, through decades of collaboration between its geologists and finance, it would be foolish to give away such a valuable capability that competitors would find difficult to match.

In addition to these strategic factors, you also need to think about your current level of operational performance. If a process's operational performance is already superior to any potential supplier, why outsource the activity? Yet even if its performance is currently below that of potential suppliers, you still might choose not to outsource the activity if you think that you could significantly improve its performance. Figure 3.3 illustrates this decision logic.

FIGURE 3.3 The decision logic of outsourcing

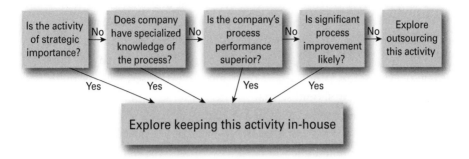

Any of the benefits of outsourcing could also, at least theoretically, be gained from in-sourcing. They are really part of the same idea. Both involve removing tasks that have traditionally been performed by you and transferring responsibility to someone else. Both are an attempt to leverage the effects of scale, focused expertise, labour arbitrage, or all three. The main difference is ownership. Outsourcing is paying someone else to do stuff for you, while with shared services you keep responsibility in-house, albeit not with you.

There are other benefits than cost savings

Yet, as experience of shared services has developed, further benefits have emerged. The standardization that is a prerequisite to consolidating services makes performance comparisons faster, easier and cheaper – or maybe even feasible for the first time. Similarly, conforming with corporate governance requirements, International Financial Reporting Standards, Sarbanes–Oxley and other requirements, becomes easier.

Another advocate of shared services, Siemens, the electronics and electrical engineering group, also stresses the importance of process improvement in responding to customers' needs. 'The result is a win-win situation,' explains Christoph Urban, CFO of Siemens in the UK and head of their Shared Services initiative. 'The customer, that is, the relevant Siemens unit, gets better quality at lower cost and can concentrate more on its core business [and] the company enjoys increased competitiveness and attractiveness as an employer.'[vii]

Why doesn't it always deliver what it promises?

Yet despite the growth of finance outsourcing and shared services, some users are surprisingly dissatisfied with their decision. One survey of global CFOs found that 54 per cent thought that outsourcing didn't deliver its promised benefits. But 73 per cent still accepted that they may be outsourcing at least some, if not all, of their finance processes. Clearly there is a paradox here. Why should so many firms continue to pursue their outsourcing option when it seems to have a patchy history? Is it a triumph of hope over experience? Or is it an indication that there are indeed valuable opportunities in outsourcing, but you need to address some significant challenges and risks if it is to be successful? For example, outsourcing may require culture change and we all know that changing an organization's culture is far from straightforward. Siemens USA had 28 different ways to pay invoices. When they started to consolidate these activities, each unit was reluctant to open its entrenched structures to a new and unfamiliar centralized unit. Luckily, they were able to overcome this, but it's fair to say it's not easy work. For them, the rewards were huge.

It could also imply that a large number of outsourcing contracts have been badly managed.[viii] Or even, to bring the elephant into the room, that outsourcing is being forced on finance by organizations keen to save costs in challenging economic times. If you don't want to do it, and you don't know how to do it well, its chances of success are slim. So we hope you find the ideas in this chapter helpful in putting you back in charge of the outsourcing agenda.

New structures, new skills

So, shared service organizations are (a) growing, (b) seemingly great at driving cost down and (c) have the potential to improve faster than processes that are distributed throughout the finance function. Yet not all examples of shared services work as well as they might. There are undoubtedly new challenges to be faced in making shared services work. Some of these challenges lie with the leadership of the shared service organizations themselves. They demand a whole new set of skills from their management teams. There are always barriers to be overcome in achieving internal improvement at the same time as maintaining service levels for internal customers. But many of the problems in making shared services a success come from the 'customer' side. In relying on internal shared services, just as in relying on outsourced services, customers need to share responsibility for managing the interface between the shared service and its own processes. Throwing an inefficient process over the wall to a shared service unit and expecting it to miraculously improve is unrealistic. Similarly, failing to specify exactly the service levels you require essentially means that you won't achieve them. The essence of successful shared service structures is through accepting shared responsibility.

Prime candidates in finance?

So which parts of the finance function's activities should be outsourced, which parts should be allocated to some kind of shared service organization internally and which parts should be kept in their traditional functional home? The answer depends on a whole set of issues that are beyond the scope of this book. So, just a signpost here. One of the main drivers is the nature of the process and in particular its volume and variety characteristics.

Very broadly speaking, very high volume/low variety processes are usually the prime candidates for outsourcing. An activity such as invoice payments, for example, is relatively common not just within an organization but across different organizations. Any one of the many business process outsourcing companies may be able to provide a superior service to our own internal efforts. For those processes with slightly lower volumes and higher variety, there may still be efficiencies to be gained from some degree of centralizing these processes, possibly in the form of an internal shared service organization.

Relatively low-volume and high-variety processes that need specialized or local knowledge are the most likely to remain within their local finance offices. However, there are exceptions. Sometimes extremely low-volume and high-variety processes, particularly if they have a high diagnostic or knowledge-based content, could be tackled by some kind of specialist unit, inside or outside the company. While not conventionally called a shared service organization, this kind of internal consultancy approach might be the best solution to keeping specialist knowledge together and developing expertise. An example here would be mergers and acquisitions (M&A). Mohit Bhatia, who we met earlier in this chapter, explains how it works for Genpact:

> We have M&A leaders in the company, with a pipeline of targets and high level analytics that produce a shortlist that goes to the board, which gives permission.

If it gets that far, the board conversation is led by the specialist M&A leader. Companies with a lower level of M&A activity might outsource this activity to an investment bank.

Let's now move on to step 3, how do you make sure that you have allocated adequate resources to ensure success?

Step 3: Resource processes appropriately

You will by now have worked out that volume and variety influence almost every aspect of process management. Processes with different volume-variety positions will have different flow characteristics, need different technologies and different approaches to designing jobs. So an early and obvious test is to check that processes with differing volume and variety characteristics are resourced appropriately. For example, processes with a low volume and a high variety of activities generally benefit little from high levels of techno-logical investment. They require relatively manual, general purpose, small-scale and flexible technologies such as spreadsheets. In contrast, processes with relatively high volumes and a low variety of activities need automated, dedicated and large-scale technologies, such as Enterprise Resource Planning (ERP[ix]) platforms. They can be somewhat inflexible, but it beats the errors you could suffer if you tried to use spreadsheets on this scale.

There's also an impact on job design. Broadly, high-variety and low-volume processes require broad, relatively undefined jobs with decision-making dis-cretion. Such jobs tend to have intrinsic job satisfaction, because people have choice and feel in control. In contrast, high-volume and low-variety processes tend to require jobs that are relatively narrow in scope and closely defined with relatively little decision-making discretion. Here, the job may not carry intrinsic motivation and you need to think how to create that.

Getting resource levels right

But what happens if processes are allocated inappropriate resources? Figure 3.4 illustrates what is sometimes called the product–process matrix.[x] The underlying idea is that many of the more important elements of process design are strongly related to the volume–variety position of the process. So, for any process, the tasks that it undertakes, the flow of items through the process, the layout of its resources, the technology it uses and the design of jobs are all strongly influenced by its volume–variety position. This means that most processes should lie close to the diagonal of the matrix that represents the fit between the process and its volume–variety position. This is called the natural diagonal.

FIGURE 3.4 The product–process matrix

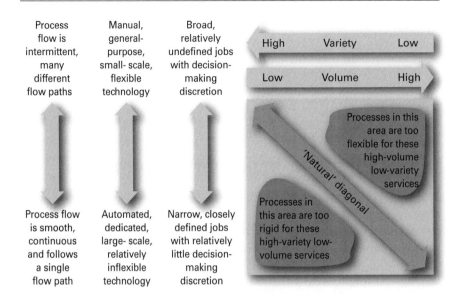

Processes lying on the natural diagonal of the matrix will normally have lower operating costs than ones with the same volume–variety position that lie off the diagonal. This is because the diagonal represents the most appropriate process design for any volume–variety position. Processes that are on the right of the natural diagonal would normally be associated with lower volumes and higher variety. This means that they are likely to be more flexible than seems to be warranted by their actual volume–variety position. That is, they are not taking advantage of their ability to standardize their activities. Because of this, their costs are likely to be higher than they would be with a process that was on the diagonal.

Conversely, processes that are on the left of the diagonal are in a position that would normally be appropriate for higher volume and lower variety processes. Processes will therefore be over-standardized and probably too inflexible for their volume–variety position. This lack of flexibility can also lead to high costs, because the process will not be able to change from one activity to another as readily as a more flexible process.

One note of caution. Although this is logically coherent, it is a conceptual model rather than something that can be scaled. Although it is intuitively obvious that deviating from the diagonal increases costs, the precise amount by which costs will increase is difficult to determine. Nevertheless, a good first test of an existing process is to check if it is on the natural diagonal of the product–process matrix. For example, the volume–variety position of the process may have changed without any corresponding change in its design. Alternatively, you may have made design changes without considering their suitability for the process's actual volume–variety position.

All this implies that, as a leader, you need to get personally involved. This leads us on to Step 4.

Step 4: Get your hands dirty in process design

Resourcing is only the beginning of process design. Within the broad parameters set out by the resources allocated to a process, there are many more detailed decisions to be made that will dictate the way materials, information and customers flow through the process. Don't dismiss these as technicalities. They are important because they determine the actual performance of the process in practice and eventually its contribution to the performance of the whole business.

You carry ultimate responsibility for how your processes are put together. Do not even consider handing over responsibility for the design of your processes to junior staff, or to internal 'experts' – and certainly not to external consultants. It's too important to delegate or outsource. After all, you will be held accountable if it all goes wrong. But there is a major difference between understanding, and taking responsibility for, process design and getting bogged down in the minutiae. Especially for activities in the mid- to low-volume range, process design is often a matter of imposing a sensible structure on the activity without constraining individual judgement, initiative or creativity. Here's how it should be done.

Leading process design as an executive

Jim Glazier is a convert to the process perspective. He heads corporate Institutional and Public Affairs (IPA) for one of the largest pulp, paper and paper products companies in Europe. His operation works with the EU's key institutions – the European Commission, the Council of the European Union, the European Parliament and all the various national governments.

Jim's greatest success since taking over IPA has been to sharpen the lobbying operation's processes, so that both productivity and effectiveness have improved. As you can imagine, this is a low-volume, high-variety, sophisticated process. So, convincing his staff had its challenges. The attitude of some staff was:

> I'm a qualified professional, I don't just follow a simple set of rules, I use my brains and my experience to make vital decisions. I'm not simply a cog in a machine. It just wouldn't work because we have to think on our feet. Our job is the very antithesis of process. Our activities are never routine or repetitive – making them into processes would take away any creativity and the job would become uninspiring and boring. It would impose unnecessary restrictions, reducing our freedom to act as we think appropriate. It would take away our humanity, even our self-worth.

Quite the revolt. Jim had to work hard to persuade his colleagues. He wanted, he said, to define exactly what the IPA unit should be doing. He argued that even skilled and experienced professionals needed to be more systematic about how they managed themselves. And the first step to systematizing the team's activities would be to define all their processes. He pledged that he would resist any move that would reduce their ability to do their job to the best professional standard.

In fact, the exercise was far more useful than even Jim had anticipated, not so much for any great revelations, but for the serious questions it posed. First, it turned out that staff members had slightly different views of the various activities that were required, as well as their appropriate frequency, their correct sequence and their relative importance. They also discussed each stage in the process and tried to assess honestly how important each activity was in contributing to their mission, how good they were at doing it and how they could improve. Jim said:

> When discussing our activities with my team, it soon became apparent that there was a clear timescale-related aspect to our work. There's a set of things that we have to do each quarter; another set that we do at the start of every week; another list that guides what we do when we are actually in Parliament; and finally a list of follow-up actions that we do, or at least should do, after the meetings. All our new process does is to make sure that we do everything we should, we know who is responsible for doing it, when it should be done, who needs to be informed and how, what resources we need and so on.
> It's not rocket science, but it works. It certainly doesn't limit our professional judgement; in fact it gives us a less unpredictable environment in which to develop our skills.

Jim's starting point was to understand how the current process operates. He mapped the process in a basic, descriptive way. He ordered the activities into various timescales. Most importantly, he has taken a critical but constructive view of how things are currently done and how they should be done.

This is just the start. For most processes we can take things further. A possible next step would be to quantify how long the various activities take, or should take. We may not be able to measure a precise activity time, but even a ballpark figure can help – and it would certainly require his team to exercise judgement. Why are some professionals reluctant to put a number on an activity or on the capacity of staff to perform tasks? Because we can never get it exactly right? Finance professionals spend their lives trying to measure things. Without some estimate of costs, times, inventories, volumes and capacity, you are missing vital pieces of the jigsaw puzzle that give you an overall picture. Without our best guesses, we are flying blind. So why don't we do this with our processes? Even rough estimates of work times, capacity, loading and variability are better than nothing. Otherwise we are at the mercy of the process, rather than managing it. And doesn't it feel like that, sometimes? It's not a comfortable feeling.

Going further into the world of process design, particularly for those running high volume finance factories, means that you will be able to leverage scale in these operations. Even asking some basic questions about how we should be doing stuff is worthwhile, as Jim and his team found out. Now to our last step, continuous improvement.

Step 5: Build in continuous improvement

Improvement comes from closing the gap between where you are and where you want to be. So, unless you are perfectly satisfied with every aspect of your processes (unlikely), look for improvement. Performance improvement is the ultimate objective of all process management; it's why we take a process perspective. Continuous improvement pops up again and again in different guises, from scientific management over a century ago,[xi] through total quality management (TQM), continuous improvement (CI), lean operations, business process re-engineering (BPR), Six Sigma and so on. All of these, and others, have something to contribute to our ideas of how to improve processes. None is the ultimate panacea, the silver bullet that guarantees perfection, but all have some merit.

The problem with these approaches to improvement is not what they contain or omit, it's what we expect from them and how we use them. Before you can judge whether any of these approaches is right for you, understand what they are, their underlying philosophy and how they differ from each other. In reality, there is considerable overlap between many of these approaches, even when their underlying philosophy differs. It is best to think of each as a toolbox that is filled with a collection of techniques. Each toolbox has different, but overlapping, techniques from a shared pool. Depending on which techniques are included, the overall philosophy of the toolbox will be different. Further, as they develop over time, they may acquire more techniques from the shared pool, or from each other. For example Six Sigma started out as a simple technical process control technique and has since adopted many other techniques into its toolbox.

To help you to understand the similarities and differences, we have mapped the different toolboxes against two criteria. The first is whether the toolbox emphasizes a gradual, continuous approach to improvement, or whether it recommends a more radical, breakthrough level of change. The second difference is whether the toolbox prescribes *what* changes should be made or emphasizes *how* changes should be made. Some toolboxes have a firm view of the best way to organize processes and resources. Others hold no particular view on what an operation should do, but concentrate instead on how the managers should decide what to do.

Figure 3.5 maps four of the most common approaches against these two dimensions. Business process re-engineering (BPR) for example is relatively clear in what it is recommending. It has a definite list of what operations' resources should or shouldn't be – processes should be end-to-end, non-value added work should be eliminated, inventory should be reduced, technology should be flexible and so on. BPR also assumes fairly dramatic change. Contrast this with both Six Sigma and TQM, which focus to a far greater extent on *how* operations should be improved. Six Sigma in particular has relatively little to say about what is good or bad in the way processes are organized, except that it emphasizes the negative effects of process variation. It concerns itself largely with the way in which improvements should be made, using evidence, quantitative analysis and a particular improvement cycle. TQM and Lean both incorporate ideas of continuous improvement, while Six Sigma is relatively neutral on this issue.

FIGURE 3.5 Mapping four common process improvement tools

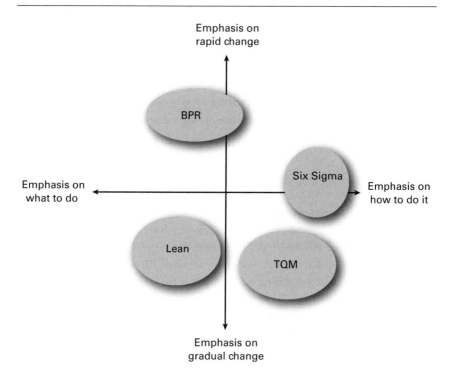

What's the message here? Choose the right tool for the job.

You have choices

It is important to understand that you have choice. By all means buy into one of the pre-packaged improvement approaches such as Lean or Six Sigma. But don't think that you have to. You always have the option of looking inside each toolbox and only taking out the techniques that you believe could work for you. Provided that the techniques don't contradict each other and that, together, they place you where you want to be in Figure 3.5, there can be advantages in customizing your own approach. This is probably especially true when you are tacking low-volume, high-variety processes, where only a highly customized approach may be flexible enough. There can also be advantage in adopting some of the same tools as the rest of your organization, if they are already in use elsewhere. Remember the two process responsibilities of CFOs, set out earlier. The first is to improve your own processes and the second is to help the rest of the organization to improve theirs. Sharing common tools and a common approach to improvement can make this a lot easier.

Summary ... and looking ahead

In this chapter we have made the case for finance to think about itself like a factory, with processes that can be mapped and improved. Whether these processes are sophisticated or routine, we believe that they can be improved, for the benefit of finance and for the benefit of the organization as a whole. We encourage you to lead this effort personally, so that you can leverage the best possible return from the investment that you make. If you like, this chapter provides you with the start of a toolkit for process improvement.

From Chapter 4 onwards, we look at how you bring together your technical finance, leadership and process management skills and apply them to your three key sources of value protection and creation: control, risk and investment.

Control – moving beyond closing the books

Is your firm under control? To what extent are you encountering surprises in operations, like safety and environmental performance, as well as in finance and other functional areas? As one of the firm's leaders, you have a role to play in identifying, and helping to resolve, control weaknesses across the business. Chapter 4 demonstrates how you can bring a control mindset to your broad finance responsibilities.

When you hear the word control, what comes to mind? For many finance professionals, control is something the accountants take care of every quarter when the books are closed. Isn't that why the lead accountant is often called the controller? We think this is a limited definition of control. We believe a control mindset is more fundamental and wide-reaching. A robust system of controls helps to ensure that all aspects of finance activity attain a predictable standard of performance, with much less performance variability.

When we ask if your finance activities are under control, we are not asking if they are perfect. Perfection is impossible. Processes do go out of kilter. A robust system of controls is something else. It assumes that your processes will wobble from time to time and calls for continuous monitoring to understand the best access points for intervention. The control mindset should apply across the whole set of finance activities – from paying the bills to M&A.

Do your business analysts scramble to ensure that vast amounts of data are more or less accurate before historical snapshots are sent to management? Or are they able to convert the data into reliable and meaningful information that provides your executive team data with strategic and tactical levers to action? That's the difference between being out of control and in control. The next chapter explains how to do it.

Notes

[i] Definition from N. Slack, A. Brandon-Jones, R. Johnston and A. Betts, *Operations and Process Management*, 3rd edition, Financial Times Prentice Hall, 2012.

[ii] Craig Wynett, Vice President and Chief Learning Officer at P&G, speaking at a London conference *Innovate to Success*, 9 May 2011.

[iii] The number of academic and professional articles on operations and process strategy is evident in journals such as *The Journal of Operations Management* and books such as *Operations Strategy*, 3rd edition, by N. Slack and M.A. Lewis, Financial Times Prentice Hall, 2011.

[iv] Tom Lester, *Understanding Shared Services*, September 2006.

[v] Hackett.

[vi] Exult corporate report, 2010.

[vii] Siemens (2007) 'Shared Services' **www.siemens.com/journal**, 15 February.

[viii] Research conducted by CFO Research Services and quoted in Alexa Michael (2008) *Outsourcing the Finance Function*, Chartered Institute of Management Accountants. Alexa Michael analyses the most important factors to consider when making decisions on outsourcing your firm's accounting processes.

[ix] Wikipedia reliably informs us that Enterprise Resource Planning (ERP) integrates internal and external management information across an entire organization. ERP systems automate this activity with an integrated software application. Its purpose is to facilitate the flow of information between all business functions inside the boundaries of the organization and manage the connections to outside stakeholders.

[x] The original idea of the product process matrix was put forward by Hayes and Wheelwright, back in 1984 in a book called *Restoring Our Competitive Edge*, published by Wiley. This is an updated version of their idea.

[xi] Engineers got their hands on organizations long before psychologists imported their ideas on motivating employees. Frederick Winslow Taylor was an American mechanical engineer who wanted to improve industrial efficiency. He is known as the father of scientific management and , as one of the first engineering consultants, achieved outstanding productivity improvements in the late 1800s, at Bethlehem Steel and elsewhere.

Establishing and maintaining robust controls

CASE STUDY A hard lesson in maintaining control

Christina, the firm's CFO, sat very still and focused on keeping her face calm. In reality, she was stunned by the executive team's harsh response to her quarterly financial review of the business.

'Why are we getting all of these accounting surprises from your team?' the COO pointedly asked. 'We have been counting inventory around the globe for years – with no concerns from any of our auditors – and now suddenly you tell me that we need to take a big write-down because the division we purchased five years ago accounts for inventory differently from the rest of our business?'

The safety and environmental officer chimed in: 'I don't believe the accident data you are collecting. We've had five very regrettable fatalities – those are hard to hide – but the underlying accident frequency and trends you are reporting look way too low relative to standard relationships between injuries and fatalities. I think the businesses are under-reporting their accidents, and I think your finance team is a passive co-conspirator!'

'And what happened to our capital spending numbers?' the General Counsel asked. 'For the last two quarters you've told us we were on track to hit the targets we shared with the market and now you say that a couple of the businesses have "recalibrated" and are going to be over budget by nearly 25 per cent? The market won't want to hear that our ability to predict our own numbers is so out of control.'

The CEO closed the meeting with a request for a review of the numbers within the week. Then he walked his CFO down the corridor and back to her office. 'What the hell's going on? Christina, you and I have been working on next week's strategy presentation to investors for over a month. Core to our presentation is our assertion that we have the resources, business relationships and technology advantages to sustain growth in our firm for the next six years. But with all of these lapses in basic data for accounting, operations and business reporting, I'm becoming very dubious that any of our strategic assertions are really true. This is very bad. At least you could have warned me before the meeting about the bombshells you were going to drop. This is not what I call an effective partnership.'

Christina sat alone in her office, wondering how she could have been so stupid as to think that the executive committee would welcome the facts. They didn't believe her and she couldn't blame them – the messages were way out of line from earlier ones. And how had she got herself into such a mess – blowing her hard-built credibility in one short meeting? She realized that all of her business training and experiences had taught her to assume internal control processes were in place. It was now clear that not only were the firm's internal control systems and processes fundamentally lacking, they were having a negative impact on other work across the entire enterprise.

Christina had to ensure that the basics were put in place. She was absolutely determined to claw the situation back and saw only a mountain of hard work ahead of her – as if the job wasn't challenging enough already. 'Well, lesson learnt', she said to herself grimly. 'I never want to sit through a meeting like that again in my life.'

Do you take control for granted?

Once you open Pandora's box,[i] it's hard to get the lid back on. So once we start looking at the assumptions and the methods of collection that underpin our numbers, we may get nasty surprises, like Christina.

We expect the basic processes in our organization to be under control, but do we realize how important control really is? Allister Wilson, the Ernst & Young partner we introduced in Chapter 1, sees losing control as the number one threat, both to an organization and to its CFO personally: 'If you lose control in the business, the consequences are huge. At the extreme, the business can lose value and even its licence to operate – and then so does the CFO.' So control lapses aren't just career limiting for the CFO, as we saw in Christina's story. If they spiral and escalate, the organization itself could be in danger. Later on, we will look at the most common, threatening control issues faced across organizations.

In this chapter we start by defining control. We next consider what stops us from doing it effectively, when it is so fundamental to value creation. (Why, like Christina, do we assume that we are in control, until it becomes apparent that we aren't?) Then we introduce a comprehensive control model that resembles a pyramid. We believe that control spans a range of levels, from the operational (internal controls) to the strategic (business reporting and planning). We take an in-depth look at what good control looks like at each of the five levels in the model. We believe that this model will offer you a comprehensive overview of the control processes you need to put in place and help you to avoid unpleasant surprises.

We will also pull lessons from process management and leadership to help you to exert control more effectively in your own organization. We believe that the CFO's role is to focus both on the tactical objectives of compliance and, perhaps even more importantly, the spirit of control. This spirit must be consistently maintained and embedded in the culture of the whole organization in order to remain strong under the acute pressure of attaining quarterly results, year-end financial objectives, integrating acquisitions and keeping ahead of the competition. Integrity is at the heart of control and the CFO's commitment to integrity must be unwavering even under duress.

Let's start by defining control.

What do we mean by control?

The 1935 edition of *Webster's* defines control as:

> 1. The act or fact of controlling: power or authority to control; directing or restraining domination; as parental control. 2. Reserved constraint. Speak without control. 3. A means or method of controlling; *specif:* (a) A controller (b) Anything affording a standard of comparison or means of verification, as an organism, culture, group, or control experiment; a check.

It's interesting how these definitions differ in tone. The first definition triggers thoughts of being bound and restricted – the second, thoughts of being personally exposed – while the third is more scientific and benign. If you have either of the first two meanings of the word in your head, it is little surprise that you inadvertently cringe at the word. What we are talking about here – an essential capability for today's world class CFO and custodian of value – works much better with definition number three, the scientific one. Wikipedia is on the same wavelength:

> Control theory is an interdisciplinary branch of engineering and mathematics that deals with the behaviour of dynamic systems. The usual objective of control theory is to calculate solutions for the proper corrective action from the controller that result in system stability, that is, the system will hold the set point (desired output) and not oscillate around it.

Controls monitor and adjust the system to obtain the desired outputs. It's like the thermostat in your house. To maintain a steady output, or temperature, from your heating, it will make adjustments when the inputs change – like cooler weather, or windows and doors left open. We want you and your finance team to act as the thermostat for your enterprise – continuously monitoring your areas of responsibility and adjusting and readjusting to keep the output constant and reliable. There are two underpinning assumptions here. The first is that things change all the time – there is no such thing as steady state. If there were, we wouldn't need a thermostat. The second is that there will be inevitable lapses in your internal systems. They will break down and you should expect this. Remember Allister Wilson's advice from Chapter 2, that there is no such thing as silent running? And you will monitor and readjust control because it is the foundation of your organization in terms of maintaining its desired value. But as ever, there may be obstacles in our path.

What stops us?

We are advocates for establishing robust controls across the enterprise, but we know that there are a number of challenges. These include how finance professionals perceive the notion of control and the, often limited, importance they assign to achieving control. We often miss the big picture in seeing how control provides the foundation to everything finance does. But if the foundation is rocky, the house could fall.

Education and attitudes can block understanding

One challenge for many finance professionals relates to their lack of direct, hands on experience with maintaining robust controls. This is especially true if you entered your firm through the MBA channel, bypassing the entry level accounting positions where control skills are really developed. For people thrown straight into business analysis, management reporting and strategic planning, your formative years were more about managing large volumes of data, honing your analytical and presentation skills and meeting impossibly tight deadlines. Worrying about whether something is in control or not was not part of this menu. In essence, you are focused on activity, instead of on controlling processes.

Another challenge is more about how we see our job, because some finance professionals see control as someone else's job. Hand on heart, do some of you think that continuously monitoring activity is frankly a bit boring compared with solving big problems? And sustaining robust controls generally isn't acknowledged or rewarded by management. It's like crime prevention – it's hard to measure and it goes unnoticed until something goes horribly wrong. And it can be hard to get your team excited about it either. They are often much more caught up in the hurly-burly of producing numbers and achieving milestones on projects. To produce something feels more, well productive, than to prevent something.

Control experts don't always help

As CFO, you may have had internal or external experts approach you with very legitimate concerns about your control framework. Unfortunately, because these experts typically are steeped in the fundamentals of control, they often aren't that curious about the essential objectives that you want to achieve. They have a tendency to dive straight into extensive presentations of the detailed and complicated systems and procedures that they are advocating. You would be forgiven for letting your eyes glaze over and swiftly delegating the work to someone more junior. The problem is – without understanding and leadership from you – the people lower down the organization will not have the power to get these important systems and controls implemented. So we would ask you to pause and think through what you need from your control systems, before you delegate their execution. If it's important to you, it will be important to your extended team and they'll want to make it work.

See it as an opportunity for learning, not blame

Your reaction as a leader to control failures is critical in determining whether you hear about lapses, and so have the opportunity to correct them, or whether they are hidden from you. Remember Douglas Flint, the Chairman of HSBC, from Chapter 2? He encourages his people to put their hand up when things go wrong, so that he has the chance to course correct. Control lapses will happen – accept it. And they provide one of the best opportunities to develop and grow as a finance professional. Even as she simmered after the executive committee meeting, Christina knew that. Our control interventions are intended to correct whatever is happening and bring it back towards the original or modified plan.

Our interventions should modify the behaviour of processes or activities. By examining, and seeking an explanation for, this cause–effect relationship, we can learn something about how our organization behaves. Even if our intervention doesn't bring the desired change, that's still a learning opportunity. It goes further. If we can share our learning with others, it should accumulate to enrich our knowledge of the underlying patterns of our organization – why things happen the way they do. And with a better understanding of the way things happen, we can target our control interventions more effectively next time.

So this logic exposes the virtuous cycle, shown in Figure 4.1. Control means intervention, intervention promotes learning, learning enhances organizational knowledge and a better understanding of how the organization operates encourages more effective intervention.

FIGURE 4.1 The virtuous cycle of intervention, learning and knowledge

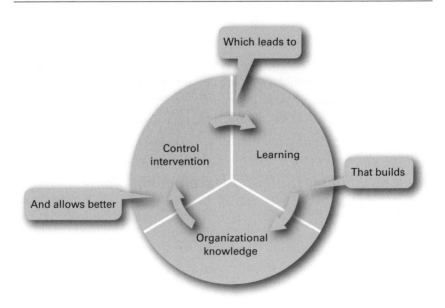

Different controls are needed for different activities at different levels. Let's look at how we can get a complete picture.

A model for managing control

Do you remember Maslow's hierarchy of needs?[ii] He suggested that humans have a hierarchy of motivations or drivers, from the most basic (food) to the most sophisticated (self-actualization, or fulfilling their potential as sentient beings through creative thought). His pyramid suggests five levels of drivers, with each level needing to be satisfied before the next, higher level can be reached.

We believe that this is the perfect model to help us to describe comprehensive control processes within an organization (see Figure 4.2). Just like human beings, you need to meet the control needs at each level, before you can reach the next. And, like Maslow, all five levels must be satisfied in order to have a robust system of comprehensive controls.

FIGURE 4.2 The control pyramid

Walking through the levels

There are five levels to the hierarchy, but there are also some harder transitions, represented by the thick black lines in the pyramid. These dark lines represent significant steps that you can't achieve until you have established the controls in the level below. These black-line distinctions are also important in building control into your organization in an effective and logical sequence.

At the bottom of the pyramid is the foundation; fundamental internal controls, without which successive layers of broader and more sophisticated control and strategic capabilities cannot be built. Internal control systems ensure that resources are acquired economically and protected from waste, loss, theft or misuse; that resources are used in accordance with laws, regulations and internal policies and procedures; and finally, that financial information is reliable, verifiable and timely.

Allister Wilson, the Ernst & Young partner we mentioned earlier, endorses the importance of these foundational controls:

> One of the biggest control issues facing international businesses today is the area of fraud and bribery. By this I mean supplier and other third party fraud, procurement fraud, product theft and bribery to get contracts. The risks facing companies are heightened by the wide reach of anti-bribery and corruption legislation in the UK and US. You need an armoury of proactive activities in place – policies alone are insufficient to maintain control.

From his vantage point working with many firms, Allister highlights for us some of the major control issues that they have in common. We'll return later to his contention that control policies won't work alone and think about what other issues you may need to tackle as a finance professional in protecting your enterprise.

Internal control moves seamlessly into the second layer of the pyramid, systems and processes. Systems and processes ensure that controls are designed, implemented and maintained through internal specifics such as organizational structure, approval and monitoring procedures and how you develop professional capability. As the thick black line suggests, without the fundamentals of internal controls and systems and processes, you won't be able to tackle more sophisticated control issues higher in the pyramid.

Operational analysis and reporting is the next level in the hierarchy. These activities focus on areas of control affected by internal and external operational issues, such as financial and business reporting, forecasting, budget variances and other performance evaluation analysis. The strength and reliability of this analysis can help to mitigate volatility in operational performance and improve how you forecast revenues and costs. The reliability and effectiveness of operational analysis and reporting requires a trusting partnership with the organization as a whole, as Christina heard loud and clear in her meeting.

Once adequate internal controls, systems and processes, and operational analysis and reporting are in place, you are ready for the next level in the hierarchy, business level reporting and monitoring. This brings a swathe of additional factors into the control space including balance sheet issues, tax, currency fluctuations, transfer pricing and capital costs. This is where internal data is translated for external audiences. External stakeholders most closely scrutinize the consistency of performance relative to historical norms, forecast guidance and competitive trends.

Finally, the strategic planning level is unattainable without satisfying all the layers below and is another thick black line transition. While strategic planning is vital to help sustain and grow the value of your enterprise, the data you use to plan can only come into focus once all the requirements lower down in the pyramid are satisfied. Simply put, there is no point in doing a lot of strategic planning if your basic internal controls are unreliable – you are building castles in the air.

Let's walk up the pyramid and explain each level and its control challenges in more detail.

Starting at the bottom – internal control

What we are talking about here is protection, compliance and reliability. Internal control has been taught for decades and most firms have numerous internal control experts. That's why our history since 2000 has been so shocking, with huge lapses in internal control that bankrupted Enron and later bankrupted Lehman Brothers and others. As the Queen (of the United Kingdom) embarrassingly asked about the financial services crisis, on a visit to the London School of Economics in November 2008, why did no one see this coming? How did things get so badly out of control?

In response to accounting scandals such as Enron, Tyco and WorldCom in the early 2000s, a slew of laws and regulations have been passed with the intention of correcting these shortcomings in control. Among them[iii] are the

Sarbanes–Oxley Act, passed by US Congress in 2002 to protect investors from possible fraudulent accounting activities by corporations; BASEL II, a set of banking regulations put forth by the Basel Committee on Bank Supervision, which regulates finance and banking internationally and sets the minimum capital requirements of financial institutions to ensure liquidity; and BASEL III, a comprehensive set of reform measures designed to improve regulation, supervision and risk management within the banking sector, largely in response to the credit crisis. But as Allister Wilson of Ernst & Young cautions, policies and legislation on their own are insufficient to prevent control lapses: 'Policies won't cut it alone. You need a proactive control framework, an effective whistle blowing policy and, people who really understand the business and can look for patterns and a corporate culture that is fundamentally geared towards control.' So such legislation only provides a good backdrop encouraging companies towards compliance. We'll return later in the chapter to the other prerequisites Allister sees, strong financial leadership and a control culture, or mindset.

Despite all the training, something fundamental has been lacking. We believe that, too often, internal control has been approached tactically instead of strategically. Tactical approaches to control often adopt the most rudimentary input–output model, while a strategic approach aligns with the virtuous cycle of control set out in Figure 4.1. Let's take a closer look at internal control.

Control intervention – attaining reasonable assurance

As CFO, you need to have reasonable assurance that internal control systems are functioning effectively and that deficiencies are quickly corrected, so that:

- the business is planned and conducted in an orderly and prudent manner
- transactions and commitments entered into have proper authority
- management is able to protect the assets and manage the liabilities of the business and ensure that appropriate provisions are made for bad and doubtful debts
- risks are monitored and controlled on a regular and timely basis and there are measures, such as segregation of duties, to minimize and correct the risk of loss from irregularities, fraud and error
- management is able to monitor liquidity, profitability and the quality of assets

- the organization is able to comply with regulatory reporting requirements in even the most challenging economic environment.

While management must establish and maintain internal control, the board of directors bears ultimate accountability. They exercise their responsibilities by approving and regularly reviewing the overall business strategies and significant policies of the firm; understanding the enterprise's major risks and ensuring that management takes the steps necessary to address them; approving the organizational structure; and ensuring that management is monitoring the effectiveness of the internal control system.

The goal of *reasonable assurance* is to find the optimal level of internal control for an acceptable level of risk and cost. Absolute assurance is cost prohibitive and subject to numerous human elements, such as human error, ethical breaches and collusion, that must be monitored but are not completely controllable. Remember, there's no such thing as perfect control.

The role of internal audit in learning

At the centre of your control universe is the internal audit team, who carry critical responsibilities to provide independent assurance of the effectiveness of the internal control systems. The quality of their staff, their independence from operating management, their reporting regimes and their ethical standards are all critical.

At a minimum, the following control functions should be managed by internal audit:

- review accounting and other records and the control environment
- assist management with identifying risk
- challenge the assumptions within control systems
- review the appropriateness, scope, efficiency and effectiveness of internal control systems
- test transactions and balances and the operation of individual internal controls to ensure that specific control objectives have been met
- review implementation of management policies
- investigate where there are areas of particular concern.

As you can see from this high-level overview, the integrity and reputation of the enterprise and its leadership are inextricably linked to the effectiveness of your internal controls. Without everyone understanding the importance of financial controls, the entire organization is potentially at serious risk. Let's move up to the next level of the pyramid.

Level 2 – systems and processes

How well are your control processes working? A qualitative but objective and easily communicated approach was provided by ISO 15504.[iv] Your internal controls and the integrated systems and processes can be evaluated against six different levels of effectiveness:

Level 0	Incomplete	Process is not implemented or fails to achieve its purpose
Level 1	Performed	Process is implemented and achieves its process purpose
Level 2	Managed	Process is established, controlled and maintained
Level 3	Established	A defined process is used based on a standard process
Level 4	Predictable	Process is enacted consistently within defined limits
Level 5	Strategic	Process is improved to meet current and projected business goals

Regular review

There are some important questions that you need to answer. Control processes only continue to work if they are interrogated frequently. Here are some useful questions you can ask:

- By what process do the board of directors and senior executives detect control weaknesses, errors and inconsistencies in financial reporting, or fraudulent activities?
- What is the approach to ensure that department or division level management review standard performance and exception reports on a daily, weekly and monthly basis?
- What is the system to assist working level teams in managing and securing access to tangible assets, including cash, database and

securities, as well as access to intangible assets such as personnel information and individual identity?

Here are some additional questions covering areas managed more directly by your finance team:

- By what process do you ensure compliance with exposure limits, to ensure that specific risk exposures determined by management or required by law or regulations are constrained?

- How do you track approvals and authorizations for transactions at specific thresholds, to ensure that appropriate levels of management and oversight are in place and to establish accountability?

- What system do you use for verifications and periodic reconciliations, to identify activities and accounts in error and to notify appropriate levels of leadership of problems or concerns?

Integrating your various processes and systems of control

Maintaining a sufficient level of transparency and internal control is particularly challenging for diverse, highly sophisticated, international enterprises. They have multiple control systems and processes, including internal monitoring and compliance management, IT systems deployment, external auditor and board oversight and regulatory and rating agency review. The CFO and finance team must integrate these elements to deliver effectively and efficiently the appropriate level of control.

If you fail to integrate your various processes and systems of control, this will undermine the higher levels of the control pyramid. It's like a surgical team conducting surgery on a patient. The patient has numerous independent systems keeping the heart pumping, the lungs breathing and the brain functioning. The surgical team must ensure that each of these life-critical systems is working effectively together before surgery starts. Without them functioning well, the surgery has a shaky base and is probably dangerous.

Taking a focused approach to process improvement

You need to identify where the greatest control risks lie in order to decide which of your innumerable processes to evaluate (you can't do everything).

Then decide how these gaps can best be closed by executing a comprehensive plan designed to establish consistent and improving processes in a standardized fashion.[v] Broad-based areas such as revenue recognition, collections and disbursements, manufacturing and distribution, health, safety and environment, engineering, quality, logistics and IT are all obvious places to start.

As described by The Institute of Internal Auditors in its various guises around the world, the organization's senior leaders must attest to the adequacy of appropriate controls:

> The assessment should clearly describe management's opinion. What is the true condition of the system of internal control at the end of the year? Is it sufficiently robust to provide reasonable assurance that material errors will either be prevented or detected? The investor should be able to read the assessment and understand whether the company has adequate controls to run the business and report the results.[vi]

Are you ready to sign?

Level 3 – operational analysis and reporting – KPIs[vii]

This section is about keeping things on track and improving. So which activities fall into this area? Business operations integrate many different functions, disciplines and areas of expertise to deliver high-quality products and services. They should aim to do so in an efficient, repeatable, transparent and reportable way. Control in operational analysis represents multiple and ongoing day-to-day processes, including purchasing and receiving, inventory controls, health, safety and environmental performance and production analysis and monitoring.

Nothing highlights the importance of controls in operational analysis better than a couple of real world examples, one good, one disastrous.

A good example of continuous improvement in control

A meaningful goal coupled with appropriate processes and controls can lead to an outstanding result. A global mining firm has used this approach to achieve world-class improvements in reducing work-related accidents over the last four years. As you know, mining is a dangerous business and safety is critical, to the individuals who work there and to the firm's continued licence to operate. They attribute much of their success in achieving this strategic priority to acute focus from every employee in the organization. They have proactively created measurements for safety, accidents, and near misses[viii] (accidents that nearly occur, but do not). They credit the timely reporting of near misses as a significant contributor to improved safety processes and lower accident results, by shining a spotlight on areas of ongoing safety risk. Now they are turning their attention to their contractors, who are lagging significantly behind. The mining company is introducing safety systems and processes to its contractors, to try to bring under control these related risks, which have previously been outside their control. A mixture of focus, visibility, transparency and reward has achieved major advances for them in bringing safety under control. Don't underestimate the power of linking control focus to the reward system.

And when it goes wrong

Data breaches are an area of great concern in the control arena, as this following extract illustrates:

> In March 2007, The TJX Companies Inc. reported that at least $45.7 million credit and debit card numbers were stolen from its computer system, officially becoming the largest single victim of identity theft in the United States ... security experts, in the months following the breach, concluded that the ... $17.4 billion retailer's wireless network had less security than many people have on their home networks as it was deficient in installing firewalls and other layers of security software that it had already purchased ... Due to these vulnerabilities, a group of hackers ... were able to hack into TJX Companies Inc.'s central database ... Once in the central database, the hackers were able to make their own accounts, send encrypted messages to one another and access TJX's confidential client information and other trade-secret data, undetected, from any internet connection in the world....
>
> Given the magnitude of the breach, the costs to the TJX Companies Inc. were more than severe. Within two months of the announcement, in early 2007, its stock price had declined approximately 13 per cent during a time when the markets were fairly stagnant. Moreover, during fiscal 2008 and 2009, TJX Companies Inc. expensed $171.5 million, an amount approximately a quarter of its annual earnings, with respect to the litigation, proceedings and investigations. Including infrastructure upgrades, total cash outflow as of June 2009 was estimated at more than $320 million dollars ... this outflow does not include reputational damages or sales losses due to a lack of customer confidence concerning the safety of their identities. The ironic part of this breach is that it would have only cost TJX Companies Inc. $2 million dollars to avoid the breach by implementing its purchased security systems.[ix]

Need we say more about paying attention to your operational controls?

Level 4 – business level reporting and monitoring

Here we are talking about translating what we do for external audiences. Business level reporting is critical not just for the credibility of the finance function, but for the entire enterprise. Producing accurate and timely business level results, and monitoring the quality and reliability of the underlying information, is highly dependent upon the three prior levels in the control hierarchy. However, business level reporting also depends on quantitative and qualitative information related to competition and market dynamics, that is, it's an activity in its own right. The challenge is further exacerbated by the need to capture all of this information in real time and extrapolate it into realistic and achievable forecasts. This raises the bar on how robust and consistent the control systems need to be at this level in the hierarchy.

Some devastating stories

The recent global financial services crisis provides a number of devastating stories about lack of control both on a micro and macro level. UBS, for example, in a follow-up Shareholder Report[x] on UBS's write-downs, reported numerous control failures, such as: 'complex and incomplete reporting, inadequate systems, and neither risk management nor the control functions had readily accessible data upon which to perform fundamental analysis of the securities in the portfolio'.

In recognition of these control weaknesses, UBS leadership undertook several changes:

> In 2008, we focused on addressing our structural and strategic weaknesses and on establishing the long-term financial stability of UBS. Activities centered on the key areas we identified as requiring change: corporate governance, risk management and control processes, the liquidity and funding framework and management compensation. As a result, 2008 saw the introduction of new organization regulations to clarify the responsibilities of the Board of Directors (BoD) and the Group Executive Board (GEB), the establishment of an Executive Committee (EC) to allocate and monitor the use of capital and risk in each of the business divisions, and the formation of a dedicated BoD risk committee. We also merged the credit and market risk functions

of the Investment Bank into a single unit led by the newly established Chief Risk Officer position.[xi]

In 2011, UBS hit the headlines again with a $2 billion rogue trading scandal. Nothing can illustrate more cogently the point we keep repeating in this chapter. Control is not a one-off fix. It needs to be revisited and sustained over time, in all areas of the business, including the quality of your leadership.

But it's not all bad news – the power of finance

Bob Gray, the CFO of UBM, helped us to define some of the dilemmas that CFOs can face through his story in Chapter 2. He is a real advocate of aligning which data are reported to the market with how the data are collected internally. He says:

> UBM has brought together a collection of largely autonomous businesses. Many of these business units serve their customers across a number of media activities. For example, TechWeb offers to our customers three media activities, in about equal proportion: Events, Online and Print. A few years ago, we chose to define our segments along the lines of these horizontal media activities, because this is how capital is allocated (each segment has a different growth and risk profile). It has also made the business more efficient, because we look at how each segment is performing as a whole, for example, how is Events doing as a segment across our business units? We can spot under-performers tucked away in a business unit, which might otherwise be cross-subsidising them from another segment. For example, grouping Data Services as a segment has allowed us to probe why our medical, trade and transport data services are all operating at different levels.
>
> The impact of aligning our internal finance data collection with external reporting requirements has effectively turned us into a matrix structure. This allows us to report best practices across segments, to align internal and external financial data (so that we don't get into any reporting muddles) and to mirror how capital is, and should be, allocated. I believe you need integrity between the external reporting and the internal management structure.

This story is relevant for a couple of reasons. The first is that it shows how business level reporting can be aligned with market needs. Collecting one set of data internally and then reorganizing it to be reported externally is both onerous and dangerous, as gaps and control lapses are more likely. We also like this story because it shows how powerful finance can be as a function. The way Bob and his colleagues collect data has had an impact on the way the whole company is structured. It has also brought with it more control (they are clearer how much they spend on what) as well as operational efficiencies.

Let's now turn to our highest level of control, strategic planning.

Level 5 – strategic planning

Is your future built on rock or sand? Strategic planning can be one of the most rewarding efforts a CFO can undertake, but this can only come into focus once the demands of all the other levels of the pyramid have been met. Without competent treatment of the internal controls, systems and processes, operational analysis and business level reporting, neither the CFO nor the organization will have long-term credibility. Lapses and exposures will continue to be disruptive to your mission to create value.

The CFO as strategist – and counterweight

Due to the unique capabilities and increasing sphere of influence of the CFO, we support the current pull for the CFO to be active in the strategy of the firm. There is ample support for this increasingly strategic role, together with some caveats that are highlighted below:

> CFOs have assumed increasingly complex, strategic roles focused on driving creation of value across the entire business. Growing shareholder expectations and activism, more intense M&A, mounting regulatory scrutiny over corporate conduct and compliance, and evolving expectations for the finance function have put CFOs in the middle of many corporate decisions – made them more directly accountable for the performance of companies.[xii]

Ernst & Young report that one of the key roles of the CFO is 'developing and defining the overall strategy for your organization'.[xiii] The report goes on to list a number of attributes for the ideal CFO, including first and foremost to be an extremely good finance professional, but together with a strong commercial sensibility, a deep understanding of the business and the ability to think strategically.

This strategic role, however, must be balanced with the core responsibilities of financial control and discipline, to make sure that the CFO is an effective support for the CEO. We heard from Douglas Flint, the Chairman of HSBC, in Chapter 2, where he gave us some advice on the CFO's role in supporting the CEO. He also told us: 'The CEO is often a visionary salesman. He is even better if he shows a grasp of the constraints on him'. It is the CFO's role to offer balance to the CEO in highlighting the constraints on the business, as well as the opportunities.

In an article in the *Financial Times* newspaper in 2010,[xiv] an audit committee chairman commented: 'There are pressures on the CEO to do acquisitions, for example. You need to have someone who is the CEO's intellectual equal to balance this. In our company, it's part of the CFO's job description and he has personal incentives to stand up to the CEO.' An American board director similarly remarked that, 'The CFO role is like a conscience – someone who can pull the CEO aside and talk to him. Acting as a counter-balance to, or the conscience of, the CEO does not qualify someone to be a CEO them-selves.' These thoughts reinforce the interplay between the differing strategic contributions of the CEO and CFO. But recall from Chapter 2, that your seat at the table is won through your capability to execute your core finance responsibilities well, including control.

Achieving control in your strategic planning – and testing your acumen

Effective strategic control requires financial understanding of the business, coupled with a commitment to report accurately and consistently the com-pany's financial health. Expectations of investors have driven finance reports to grow to include progress towards publicly stated goals, operational metrics and material issues consistent with regulatory requirements. Insufficient consistency or transparency in strategy presentations can reduce investor confidence and affect the share price. The finance team needs to be intimately involved in assisting and partnering with the business as strategy is developed, to sustain controls over this process. The CFO in particular must participate in setting the strategic direction of the firm and ensuring that appropriate controls are in place to execute the strategy.

A great test of your financial and business acumen is your ability to question any aspect of your control system, including those related to your strategic planning, until you are comfortable with the answers you get. If you are uncomfortable with the answers, then you should be able to guide a team to correct the inadequacy. To be really comforted by the answers you get, you should be able to cite tangible evidence that the controls are indeed real and effective. Your standards on both counts should be slightly higher than those of your board audit committee and external auditors. While as CFO you often negotiate with your independent auditors on various subjective accounting treatments, for you, control should be non-negotiable.

As you might expect, the control of strategic planning comes back to balancing a dilemma. As competition has become fiercer and globalization continues to squeeze margins, shareholders increasingly demand sustainable, profitable growth accompanied by equally strong controls. These demands require increased capabilities, rapid assimilation of mountains of accurate and timely information and thorough analysis. Capabilities such as these are in short supply in most companies and the CFO and finance teams have a unique opportunity to fill this gap.

We have added leadership insight throughout the chapter, through our stories and quotes. Let's turn now to see how a process approach can help us to institute and manage control at all five levels of our pyramid.

A basic model of process control

At a very basic level, the control of any financial process can be seen as how we correct deviations from a previously agreed plan. So control starts with a plan, or at least some idea of what should be happening. Each part of the plan has to be monitored to check that planned activities really are taking place as intended. Any deviation from the plan can then be rectified through some kind of intervention in the process, which itself will probably involve some replanning.

Figure 4.3 illustrates this simple view of control. The output from a process, for example the number of transactions per period, is monitored and compared with the plan. The plan tells us what the process is supposed to be doing, such as the total number of transactions expected to be processed in the period. Deviations from this plan are taken into account through a replanning activity. The necessary interventions are made to the process, such as to approve more work hours or improve the quality of the input data, which will hopefully ensure that the new plan succeeds. This process review is iterative.

FIGURE 4.3 A simple model of process control

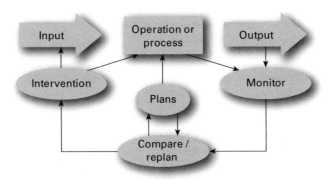

This is a good start, but it's too simple. It is a gross generalization of a far more messy reality. It's based on how mechanical systems such as car engines are controlled. But anyone who has worked in real organizations knows that they are not machines. They are social systems, full of complex and ambiguous interactions. They are political entities where different and often conflicting objectives compete and it's not always straightforward to measure outputs. Also, some decisions do not involve repetitive considerations, for example, there are one-off deals. So how can we help controllers to be truly in control?

More sophisticated control operations

So, if the control model in Figure 4.3 is too simple for all but the most basic processes, which conditions make controlling processes more complicated and how can these control challenges be met? Here are some useful questions which can be used to assess the degree of difficulty associated with control of any process:

- Is there consensus over what the process' objectives should be?
- How well can the output from the process be measured?
- Are the effects of interventions into the process predictable?
- Are the process' activities largely repetitive?

One way in which these questions may influence the nature of control is shown here in Figure 4.4 in a more sophisticated model.[xv] We then spell out what is denoted by each of these types of control in more detail, working up from the bottom of the model.

FIGURE 4.4 Decision tree for types of control

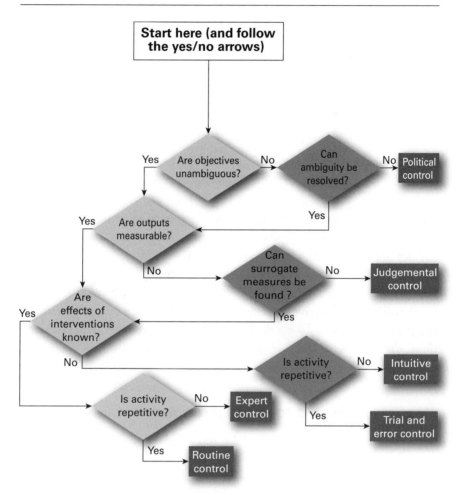

Routine control

This is the easiest case, with unambiguous objectives, measurable outputs, known effects of interventions and repetition. It applies to most current operations in production. Control here can be codified using straightforward decision rules. Here, then, the simple control model in Figure 4.3 would still work and we are probably operating at the bottom of our control pyramid in Figure 4.2.

Expert control

If objectives are unambiguous, outputs measureable, effects of interventions known but the activity is not repetitive, such as the introduction of a new

IT system, it makes sense to entrust control to an expert. Because the expert does the same work a lot, similar circumstances really are repetitive and the expert has been able to learn from experience. Just beware – experts are good at what they know, but are not always aware of the broader context for their decisions. For this type of control to be effective the expert's knowledge must be integrated with that of the regular managers for the process, who understand its context.

Trial and error control

When objectives are unambiguous, outputs are measurable and the activity is repetitive, but the effects of intervention not known, in these circumstances control becomes a learning activity. Managers learn through previous successes and failures. Post hoc analysis of the control intervention is needed to build up knowledge, which may eventually result in routine control. An example here would be budgeting processes.

Intuitive control

If objectives are unambiguous, outputs measurable, but neither the effects of the interventions are known, nor is the activity repetitive, process control becomes more of an art than a science. Individuals who possess an innate feeling for the situation, perhaps built up through experience, may be able to decide on an appropriate intervention intuitively. Such individuals are likely to need analytical skills, managerial sensitivity and detailed yet generic understanding of process behaviour. Some processes that allocate resources to new projects in large organizations are like this, especially when decisions depend on suggestions and plans developed at lower levels in the organization, but are decided upon by more senior management. Each suggestion or plan developed at a lower level is a non-repetitive activity. Attempting to get them approved is a process, where the effects of interventions are not known. This is why we need regular reviews of the process used by senior management as plans and suggestions are formulated. In effect it moves the control activity towards more of a trial-and-error type.

Judgemental control

This is probably the greyest area, in that we think we are in decision-making territory, but there are probably too many unknowns. Here objectives are unambiguous, but outputs are not measurable and there are no satisfactory indirect measures. If substitute measures can be agreed by all stakeholders, the control problem shrinks to the case of measurable output. However, if no substitute measures are acceptable to everyone, process control becomes a matter of subjective decision making. Exerting control will depend on the power and influence of the decision-maker(s). It could be argued that most strategic decisions are like this, so we are now towards the top of our control pyramid in Figure 4.2.

Political control

When objectives are ambiguous, control is particularly difficult. And objectives in many high-level decision processes are often uncertain. The reasons for such ambiguity could be because there are conflicts of interests or values between decision stakeholders, there may be lack of agreement over whether the means justify the ends, or environmental turbulence or uncertainty lead to different projections.

How does this help in control?

Basic controls are simple and we pay attention to them. More sophisticated controls are much more challenging. Without a model for approaching them, we may ignore them, manage them by diktat, or assume that someone else is taking care of them. This model is perfect to take your team through a sophisticated conversation about controlling activities that you might have thought were beyond control. It means that nothing is off the control agenda, even in circumstances when some of your colleagues might argue that only judgement or common sense would work. It makes your control framework more comprehensive and reduces the possibility of lapses.

The message here is simple but important. Different circumstances need different approaches to control. Adopting the same approach to controlling, say, an invoice payment activity as you use for complex M&A activity, just cannot make sense. This more complex control model means that we can exercise the appropriate level of control even for sophisticated and knowledge-rich processes. And repetition is also important; fixing it once and then neglecting it is a control risk in its own right.

Finally, we consider your role as a leader in building robust control processes.

You need to develop your own control expertise

There is no substitute for your own deep financial understanding, whether putting in place financial controls to meet regulatory requirements, or linking financial metrics to operational performance, or ensuring that the internal controls, systems and processes at the base of your control pyramid are working well. Recent history shows that you can't rely on others' financial expertise.

We all know stories where regulators, rating agencies and investment analysts have invested untold sums hiring financial experts to analyse and evaluate companies' financial health. Take for example the rise and fall of Tyco International in the United States. It was one of the most closely followed companies of its era. The competition watched them, dozens of analysts followed them, rating agencies and debt covenants provided ongoing monitoring, media outlets wrote numerous stories on the company and its management, auditors signed off on annual reports. There was a huge external spotlight on them. And, after dozens of acquisitions and a huge increase in their share price, Tyco International CEO L. Dennis Kozlowski was acknowledged in *Business Week*'s list[xvi] of top 25 corporate managers of 2001. But less than six months later, on 3 June 2002, he unexpectedly resigned from his CEO position. By 12 September the same year, there was a criminal indictment accusing him and CFO Mark Swartz of corruption for allegedly stealing hundreds of millions of dollars from Tyco. A jury ultimately found them guilty of stealing more than $150 million.

How did it happen? The scrutiny of publicly traded companies is immense but can never substitute for ethical leadership, constant monitoring and robust controls. Even after the introduction of numerous new regulations around the world, financial scandals are still alive and well. Scandals such as Parmalat in Italy, Bernie Madoff in the USA and Satyam Computer Services in India reinforce the need for controls to be in the fibre of the organization. As these stories demonstrate, analysis by an outsider can be flawed, inadequate and potentially misleading. You often have no way of knowing.

Creating the control DNA

So neither increased regulation, nor individual financial acumen, is sufficient to ensure adequate control across all your activities. You cannot be everywhere at once. Good control awareness and practices must be complemented by a sense of shared, enterprise wide responsibility for control. You need control in your DNA. We called this the control spirit at the start of this chapter. This is a leadership issue across all levels of the control pyramid. Is it possible to create a culture of control?

We met Mohit Bhatia, the CFO of Genpact, in Chapter 3. He is the kind of CFO you admire. He reels off figures that are immediately comprehensible and in 10 minutes can give you an overview of the company. He also knows to the rupee and dollar how much the different parts of his finance function cost (and it spans the full house from investor relations to compliance), in total and as a percentage of business expenditure. He also knows what each part of the function is achieving for the business. Roughly 50 per cent of his costs are in control accounting and cash management. Accounting, control and compliance are expected to work like clockwork. Ensuring this level of performance takes a lot of effort – so he invests in systems and processes to provide more real-time information to customers. And because his company does acquisitions and structures a variety of deals, he also provides the structure and decision criteria for his firm's commercial transactions – another form of control – as well as the data on how his firm is doing by product and by industry to inform operational decisions.

He is a great believer in Six Sigma and Lean in establishing a culture of control – but he also believes in the softer side of creating the control DNA:

> 52,000 people are responsible for our brand. We have values and we have corporate communications on integrity and publicly announce any departure from our ethics. We have an internal audit function of 25–30 people checking on employee malpractices.

Who is responsible for the culture?

Collectively, the board of directors and senior management are formally responsible for establishing a culture that demonstrates to everyone the importance and centrality of internal controls. As Mohit tells us, a culture of control includes a strong ethical environment and unwavering values of integrity, as well as training, methods for reviewing control and the role and responsibilities of internal audit. It's also important to have sound human resource policies to reward the right behaviours, covering performance management, compensation and incentives.

The consumer product giant, Procter and Gamble, demonstrated its commitment to establishing a culture of control via this statement in its 2009 annual report:

> Every employee – from senior management on down – is required to be trained on the Company's Worldwide Business Conduct Manual, which sets forth the Company's commitment to conduct its business affairs with high ethical standards. Every employee is held personally accountable for compliance and is provided several means of reporting any concerns about violations of the Worldwide Business Conduct Manual.[xvii]

Is it working? Two qualitative tests of your firm's control culture

This is a very simple test. Ask yourself how comfortable you would be going on holiday where there is no contact with your company as you close your books for the quarter. That's right – closing the quarter without your input. Not closing a month, as this should be fairly routine, and not closing the books for the year, as your financial expertise and strategic perspective would be absolutely required. So, how comfortable do you feel, on a scale of 1 to 10? If your score is 5 or less, then it is almost inevitable that there will be a significant control error. If your score is 6 to 8, you have more work to do around the fundamentals. If your score is 9 or higher, you are probably more focused on improving effectiveness and have more time to spend on your strategic impact on the business. Good for you!

A second test is to assess how quickly, in days, you can close a month, a quarter or a year – not just with speed, but also with confidence. Think about your answers and then list both what has an impact on the time period to close, as well as the reasons for your current level of confidence. Your assessment is likely to shed some interesting light on basic control issues.

Summary ... and looking ahead

Lack of control is a disaster waiting to happen. Your challenge is to maintain a robust control environment and to embed a culture of control in your organization. Control requires you to adhere diligently to established policies and procedures and to commit to ongoing improvement of control processes. Control also presents an opportunity to take compulsory, resource-intensive tasks and recast them to leverage your resources to achieve enhanced value protection and creation. The ability to sustain these efforts is significantly enhanced when control expertise, leadership capabilities and process skills are fully integrated.

Let's close this conversation by suggesting some helpful questions for finance and across your organization:

- Do you know what is really happening and is it what you actually expected?
- How do you know? Do you use anecdotal information, or are you continuously monitoring where you are headed?
- How do you intervene to correct things that deviate from what you expected?
- To what extent do you allow your business analysts to invest in systems and processes to create and sustain tools that provide competitive advantage for the firm? Or do you hold them to basic spreadsheets and incremental approaches to reduce cost and prolong legacy systems beyond their productive lives?
- How do you know your interventions are effective and not causing other deviations?
- What kind of a control environment have you created?

An unsatisfactory answer to any of these questions becomes a case for action to improve your control environment.

In 2009, Procter and Gamble reported:

> Our system of internal controls includes written policies and procedures, segregation of duties and the careful selection and development of employees. The system is designed to provide reasonable assurance that transactions are executed as authorized and appropriately recorded, that assets are safeguarded and that accounting records are sufficiently reliable to permit the preparation of financial statements conforming in all material respects with accounting principles generally accepted in the United States of America. We monitor these internal controls through control self-assessments conducted by business unit management. In addition to performing financial and compliance audits around the world, including unannounced audits, our Global Internal Audit organization provides training and continuously improves internal control processes. Appropriate actions are taken by management to correct any identified control deficiencies.[xviii]

Can you say the same?

Risk and value creation

In Chapter 5, we turn to the role of risk in creating and sustaining value for the enterprise. Taking risk is the very essence of being in business. By going into business, you raise capital, pay taxes and file accounts and so enter the realm of regulatory and statutory compliance, with penalties for non-compliance. Your firm operates businesses, often in multiple countries, and often under a variety of partnerships, all with the most positive of intentions, but not all successful. And you face competitors looking for weaknesses to exploit.

As CFO you need to be well tuned to risk management. Having periodic reviews of your checklist of risk exposures is no bad thing. And making sure you have adequate loss insurance is also an important task. But we believe you need to go further than these basic steps. You need to extend your thinking to convert risks to opportunities. And once you have incurred a serious risk, and stopped the initial damage, how do you begin to recover and move forward? To what extent are you engaging externally with CFO peers to review important risk management issues?

In Chapter 5, we will look at ways that you can enhance your risk management mindset, to ensure that you sustain and create value, rather than letting it seep away.

Notes

i An artefact from Greek mythology, the box was actually a large jar given to Pandora, which contained all the evils of the world. Her god-given curiosity compelled her to open it and release evil into the world.

ii 'A Theory of Human Motivation', by A.H. Maslow, *Psychological Review* (1943) 50(4): 370–96. The groundbreaking psychologist, Abraham Maslow, suggested that it is only once more basic human needs are met (such as the need for sustenance and physical safety),that humans can aspire to higher order needs, like forming social networks and being creative. While the idea of a hierarchy is challenged by some psychologists today, it remains popular as a simple means of distinguishing between different human motivations.

iii For more details, visit investopidia.com

iv Adapted from *ISO 15504 Conform Internal Financial Control Assessment* by János Ivanyos, Memolux Ltd (H) IIA Hungary.

v The importance of this standardized approach has been codified into law – such as Sarbanes–Oxley and other legislation listed earlier in this chapter.

vi   The Institute of Internal Auditors provides a thorough treatment of the internal control process in the publication *SARBANES-OXLEY SECTION 404: A Guide for Management by Internal Controls Practitioners*, The Institute of Internal Auditors 2nd Edition, January 2008.

vii   Key Performance Indicators.

viii   In fact, paying attention to deviations and near misses is an important part of getting back on track and keeping under control. See *How to Avoid Catastrophe*, by Caroline Tinsley, Robin Dillon and Peter Madsen, *HBR* April 2011.

ix   *Relation between Internal Control over Financial Reporting and Internal Control over Operations: Evidence from Privacy Breaches*, by Lawrence, Minutti-Mezza and Vyas, 2010. An excellent study of data breaches and how they result from a lack of operational and financial controls.

x   18 April 2008 Shareholder Report on UBS's Write-Downs available **www.ubs.com**

xi   Letter to Shareholders in the 2008 Annual Report.

xii   McKinsey & Company, March 2008.

xiii   Ernst & Young 2010 survey and report, *The DNA of the CFO*.

xiv   FT.com, 'Why do so few CFOs become CEOs?', by Anthony Goodman, Published: 1 June 2010, 13:20.

xv   G.H. Hofstede 1981, 'Management Control of Public and Not-for-Profit Activities', *Accounting, Organizations and Society* (1981) 6(3): 193–211.

xvi   *Business Week*, 14 January 2002.

xvii   Available on the Procter and Gamble website **www.pg.com**

xviii   In their 2009 annual report, Procter and Gamble provided a section entitled '*Management's Responsibility for Financial Reporting*', signed by both the CEO Bob McDonald and CFO, J.R. Moeller.

Deepening and spreading risk management

In a 2010 Ernst & Young[i] survey of 669 senior finance professionals in Europe, the Middle East, India and Africa, 63 per cent of respondents believed that improving risk management was more of a priority when compared to three years ago. The only process that was viewed as a higher priority was cash management.

CASE STUDY   Risk creeps up on you

Susan sat alone in her office behind a closed door. Her firm had just suffered a series of setbacks with regulatory authorities and the rating agencies. Now, the flagship acquisition she and others had touted to the market was being put up for sale, triggering a major write down. There were some irregularities associated with the deal and she and her head of mergers and acquisitions were under personal investigation for potential civil and criminal infractions. She felt slightly sick.

With the benefit of 20/20 hindsight, Susan could see how it had all happened. She had been recruited as CFO two years ago to bring fresh talent to the executive table and to rebuild a finance team whose professional capability was lagging. She had tried hard to lay the foundation for long-term success. She had travelled extensively to get to know her distributed finance team, encouraging them to make a more important contribution to the organization's success. She had worked actively with the executive team, the board and investors in a concerted effort to help close market capitalization gaps with the competition. She had all the strategic aspects in her sights.

In retrospect, while the big pieces had seemed to be going well, she could see how progress had been unravelled by a series of seemingly minor items. When she arrived two years ago, she remembered seeing a report from the external auditors criticizing the company's reliance on spreadsheets, and recommending a shift to hard-wired systems. But the cost and employee time needed to make the changeover never seemed a high enough priority. And then just this week, the company's auditors had detected some serious formula errors in the spreadsheets. She knew where this was headed – to a restatement of the financial books for the past two years and a very embarrassing press release.

Then there was the long-term debt package, bequeathed to her by her predecessor. This had required her Treasury team to refinance 80 per cent of the firm's debt within a single month, coincidentally the same month when the markets were being hit by a series of setbacks on the Continent. To her surprise, at exactly the same time, three of the firm's major factories had to close for retrofitting because of quality control lapses. The division manager for the three factories was claiming a confluence of unpredictable events. Susan had checked and could see that the evidence predicting the major shutdowns was right there in the management information data – once it was looked at in the right way. The convergence of internal and external uncertainty had led to a downgrade from the rating agencies.

Susan knew it would be no use explaining that these reporting and debt crises had dominated her attention, so she had spent less time ensuring robust due diligence on the acquisition than she would have liked. That would still come out in the wash-up. As it turned out, the VP championing the deal had failed to disclose some material issues and risks, so the ink was barely dry on the deal before all the bad news started coming in. Her instinct had told her that the deal didn't make financial sense. But she had let her CEO get away with the claim that shareholders would overlook the petty details and see the strategic logic in the deal. Now she was the one who was going to get it in the neck.

Susan quietly asked herself, 'Why didn't I pay closer attention to managing risk? These challenges are coming from everywhere.'

Risk management – the complement to robust controls

In Chapter 4, we outlined the essential elements for maintaining a control environment – strong internal controls, systems and processes, consistent operational and business reporting and robust strategic planning. Sustaining a control environment is a bit like being a gardener – you can work hard to set things up, but it needs ongoing attention to keep it looking good.

But things will still go wrong. Market forces, the weather, organizational complexity, human error, mechanical breakdown and even criminal behaviour lurk just beyond your internal control systems. That's why we need to add the discipline and rigour of risk management. It picks up where control can't venture.

In this chapter, we will start by defining risk and then look at how control and risk complement each other. Next, we look into why risk falls lower down our to-do list than it should and some of the barriers that we face in managing risk effectively. We then look at a four-step process for managing risk proactively and instilling a risk management mindset into the organization. The four steps are risk identification, risk prevention, risk mitigation (how we reduce the fallout from something going wrong) and risk recovery, or how resilient we can be in picking ourselves up after a calamity. Our approach is to assume we should work as hard as possible on prevention, but we should also be prepared for a speedy recovery when things go wrong.

Let's look first at risk and its relationship with our control responsibilities.

How we define risk

The 1935 edition of Webster's[ii] offers this simple definition of risk: 'a hazard; danger; peril; exposure to loss, injury, disadvantage, or destruction'. Sounds about right. Wikipedia suggests:

> Risk is the potential that a chosen action or activity (including the choice of inaction) will lead to a loss (an undesirable outcome). The notion implies that a choice having an influence on the outcome exists (or existed). Potential losses themselves may also be called 'risks'. Almost any human endeavour carries some risk, but some are much more risky than others.

These definitions suggest danger and loss. So we would like to embellish these definitions with one further thought.

Risk is about upside as well

There is a flipside to risk. Organizations must take calculated risks to earn acceptable returns. It is absolutely true that risk is not just a downside experience. Risk can also create opportunities. In fact, business exists to exploit risks in order to create shareholder value. However, to keep our narrative a bit more digestible, in this chapter we will focus on managing downside risk. We'll get to the upside opportunities that risk offers in Chapter 6.

How control and risk management fit together

Risk management is the strategic parallel to having a sound control system – the two work together like your biceps and triceps. If control is about constantly checking your processes and looking ahead, then risk management is about scanning around yourself in ever expanding arcs and creating processes to sustain this scanning. Figure 5.1 illustrates this symbiotic relationship.

FIGURE 5.1 The relationship between risk and control

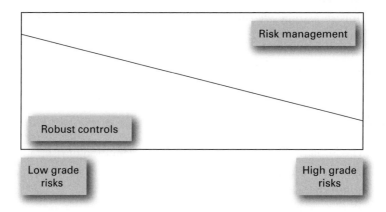

Where does control play best? Lower grade risks, where objectives are unambiguous, outputs are measurable, the effects of intervention are known and the activity is repetitive (check back to Figure 4.4 in Chapter 4), can mostly be managed through robust controls. An example would be invoice processing operations, where you need to make sure all requests for payment are evaluated for validity, paid in a timely way and properly recorded in the accounts. Of course there's risk here, but if you have robust controls in place, you should catch it. Additionally, staff might not be getting adequate training or there might be exposure to fraud – but a comprehensive control system should pick these up too.

The exception might be where cumulative and/or simultaneous lower grade risk events conspire suddenly to create a catastrophe. Simultaneous failures in redundant systems leading to meltdowns at nuclear facilities (like the Fukushima Daiichi nuclear disaster in March 2011[iii]) or multiple human errors resulting in plane crashes often result from a series of small errors rather than a single large one. So control systems also need to look for inter-connectivity between risks across the systems they safeguard.

Here's where we segue to risk. For higher grade risks, where there is more uncertainty about objectives generally and where the consequences of any single risk are much higher, the ability to manage through a system of controls is more limited. It's for these higher grade risks that you need to rely more on a well-established risk management mindset. You need an organization to support you that has an appetite for proactively scanning for, and learning about, potential risks. Such higher grade risks can be inherent in your firm's business model, such as the potential for a calamitous operational failure in a large plant. Or, they can be due to a specific set of circumstances, like human error from people overly familiar with their tasks, or new to the job.

In finance, these higher grade risks can arise from major new investments – in new lines of business, in new technologies, in new countries – and in new deals (both buying and selling). Natural catastrophes, such as the earthquake which triggered a series of lower risk but cumulatively disastrous failures at the Fukushima Daiichi plant; macroeconomic changes; disruptions in supply chains; and geopolitical events all show that circumstances beyond your firm's control can also have devastating effects. You can't control or even prevent them, but you have to be poised and ready to recover from them fast. This is a specific step in the risk management cycle.

It's your job as a custodian of value

Risk management is even more important in today's business environment. Increased globalization, squeezed margins, rapid technological advances, data breaches, continued economic uncertainty and climate change are just a few of the challenges that come to mind. There is also the ongoing chal-lenge of finding new ways to grow during an extended period of low growth in developed economies. As a custodian of value, the CFO is increasingly central to a company's competitive success and this needs to include a holistic, ongoing, end-to-end review of risk.

Let's hear again from Bernard Katompa, our CFO turned CEO at Liberty Africa:

> The CFO has to help the organization make the right call on the quantum of risk to undertake. You can choose to eliminate some risks by exiting or selling that part of the business. Where you decide to retain risk in the business, you had better have good preventative and detective controls in place. You can also choose to transfer risk to a third party (through insurance, hedging, derivatives and so on). In this case, you have to make sure that the premium you pay is lower than the likely return to your organization.

This is a great example of a risk management mindset, where the choice of which risk to eliminate or undertake and mitigate is deliberate, with the CFO playing a pivotal role. Here, Bernard offers us options on how to handle risk, which we will revisit later in the chapter.

Regrettably, in the urgency of everything else you have to do, risk management is often not fully developed, deployed, or at the top of your priority list. The worst case is probably where you have limited risk coverage in place and delude yourself that you are safe. As Einstein put it:, 'Everything that can be counted does not necessarily count; everything that counts cannot necessarily be counted.' Covering just the obvious leaves you vulnerable to the unexpected. Let's think about why we may not be as good at mitigating risk as we might hope.

Why common risk approaches fail

We all know that managing risk should include keeping checklists, updating your risk matrix, buying insurance and a whole lot more. It should be a mindset – a state of awareness. As CFO, how do you think about risk? And how do you embed in the organization a risk mindset appropriate for today's business world? There are some common pitfalls.

Not another black swan

Historically, some of us have been taught that to manage risk we must combine the probability of loss with its impact. This encourages us to run numbers and pay attention to the bigger numbers. According to this line of reasoning, the higher the probability and the bigger the impact, that's where we should be paying attention. In our view, this is insufficient. We would argue that when the impact of the outcome is large enough it trumps probability, so whether the probability is high or low, we should be paying attention to it. Allister Wilson[iv] agrees:

> I find that after a calamity, we are able to rationalize what happened by referring to black swan[v] events, or exhort the perfect storm[vi] or an unpredictable chain of events. But when you look into it, it turns out to be about how risk was viewed and managed. So-called black swan events are often entirely foreseeable, not just with the benefit of hindsight. You need to identify possible risk (including high impact, low probability risk), understand it, decide what action you will or won't take, manage it, monitor it and communicate it. And you can't look at risk in silos. There needs to be a lot more transparency in the way that risk is managed.

Susan, our disguised CFO in the opening story, had exactly this insight about the factory closures being presented as unexpected. She worked out that her organization had the information predicting them all along.

So if you find yourself caught unawares and blaming the fates, think again. Just like when you have a bad day, you can assume a series of random events, or you can look at yourself and ask what is going wrong – am I extra tired, stressed or what? There may be an underlying cause. It's the same with risk.

Just avoid mistakes?

A simple cause of failure in the way we handle risk is thinking that you can manage it by avoiding mistakes. Sure, some obvious mistakes can be avoided, like having inaccurate data in your tax returns, using unsound assumptions in investment evaluations and making accounting policy decisions that get a qualified opinion from your auditor. You can even avoid errors of omission, such as insufficient casualty insurance coverage, inadequate testing of down-side sensitivities in an investment case, or failure to back up your records in the event of a disaster. Unless you guard against basic mistakes, you will be plagued by them. But avoiding mistakes is more about maintaining quality than about managing risk. It's the equivalent of playing not to lose as opposed to playing to win. You must have a good defence, but also a good offence if you are going to win regularly in the long term.

Spread your risks

This sounds like a more sophisticated approach, doesn't it? We are all taught that return is commensurate with the amount of risk taken and that building a portfolio of opportunities with a range of riskiness can help us stay on the efficient investment frontier. With the right mix, we can maximize our return per unit of risk. That's why we say, 'don't put all your eggs in one basket'. Firms diversify their types of investment into different parts of a value chain, in different political jurisdictions and in different lines of business. They work with a spread of suppliers, partners and customers, to avoid over-dependence on the viability of any one stakeholder. And spreading your risk is exactly the right thing to do.

But as you build your portfolios, do you really understand the risk underlying each of them? If spreading risk is just one aspect of your proactive risk management, the answer is probably, yes. But if you are just hoping that a spread will yield better than expected outcomes and hedge against unexpected risk exposures, it's a bit like crossing your fingers for luck. Inadvertently, you still may be exposing your organization to significant unintended risk. If this is your approach, then you have not achieved true risk management – it's more like spread betting, or relying on a good following wind.

A narrow and linear view?

In terms of risk awareness, some finance professionals restrict themselves to assessing and managing only financially-oriented risks, like credit exposure, exchange rates and tax rates. Of course, you have to take care of the basics. But it's important for finance to manage risk holistically, including risks to delivering your business objectives and the strategy. As Allister Wilson cautions, risks don't always come in neat self-contained packages and seldom linked only to one business silo. They can interact with each other to create a bigger risk or a mess.[vii] The delicate interdependencies of seemingly unrelated factors, like the suicide in Tunisia that created a cascade of civil unrest across the Middle East and North Africa in 2011,[viii] are exacerbated in a globally networked world, where information flows freely and fast. Creeping risks can create havoc. They emerge over time and their impact can be underestimated until it's too late to change the outcome.

Allister Wilson also believes that: 'Ultimately, safety and operational risk is the same as financial risk, because you can lose your licence to operate, so finance needs to pay attention to risk across the business'. So if you want to get ahead in finance, you need to be agile across all areas of business risk. This includes the underlying risks of operational performance such as cost, production and schedule exposure. Think about political risks including changing legislative and regulatory policies; try to foresee supply chain risks like quality and delivery of critical materials; and reputation risks such as your environmental and safety performance and community relations' activities. Don't assume that your suppliers are compliant in managing their own risks, or that regulatory bodies are monitoring the overall system beyond the volumes of mandatory rules they have created. In fact, assume as little as possible.

Be alert to a wide spectrum of risk. Adopt a risk mindset, a bit like Inspector Clouseau.[ix] Remember what we said in Chapter 2 about the courage you need as a CFO leader? Being able and willing to say the unpopular and out the elephant in the room? It is not enough to avoid conflict by shaking your head quietly in the top meetings when you see operational and reputational risk being overlooked. As a custodian of value, you need to be a proactive risk manager. All risks accumulate or translate into potential harm to the reputation and value of your organization.

Failing to perceive risk in the first place

There is a human tendency to focus on the risks you already know. How can you surface organizational blind spots or uncertainties that extend beyond the visibility of your business or industry? What are your unknown unknowns?[x] It is very difficult to manage what you can't see and to be distracted by the big obvious flashing lights on the risk dashboard. This is one of the reasons that we suggest you create an active external network for yourself. Others may alert you to a risk that you currently don't see. Lift your head above the urgency of the short term to tease out these blind spots and uncertainties. Identify low probability, high impact events and avoid thinking that they can never happen. Have they happened somewhere else, perhaps in another industry? Even as an analogy for what could happen in your own business?

Let's now look at a model that can help us to monitor and manage risk in a systematic way.

The risk management process cycle

Risk management should not be a once-a-year exercise, but part of the overall business strategy. Just ask Susan, the chastened CFO in our opening story. So far in this chapter we have examined how risk relates to control and why CFOs and other finance professionals are often challenged to manage enterprise risk holistically. It's a large undertaking and not just for the CFO and the finance team. One way to embed an appropriate risk management mindset is to take a consistent and disciplined approach that is visible to everyone.

Risk and resilience

An effective risk mindset looks at both risk and resilience, as two halves of the same issue. Risk is what might happen, the 'potential unwanted negative consequences from events'. Resilience is what you can do about it, the ability to withstand and recover from those events. In practical terms, proactive risk management involves four sets of activities. The first is to identify risks by understanding what could go wrong. The second is to look for ways of preventing things going wrong. The third is risk mitigation through minimizing the negative consequences of things that have gone wrong. Finally, risk recovery means having plans and procedures to pick yourself up again when things have gone wrong, as they inevitably will. See it, stop it, minimize it, bounce back.

FIGURE 5.2 A system for proactive risk management

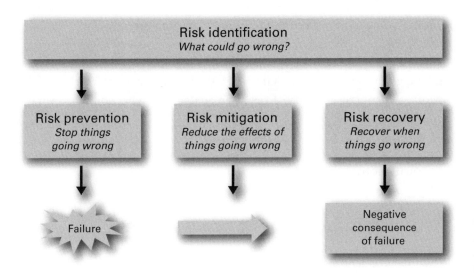

So, risk identification, risk prevention, risk mitigation and risk recovery are the four steps in the risk management cycle. The cycle loops back on itself, so that learning from an event can translate into better identification, prevention and mitigation in the future. We are encouraging you again to be the kind of leader where it's OK to admit a mistake, so that everyone can focus on fixing it and learning from it. If your team feels safer hiding it from you, it's bound to happen again.

We will examine each of the steps in the cycle. The biggest trick is probably to identify the risk in the first place – to see it.

Step 1: Risk identification

Susan overlooked the cumulative risk arising from spreadsheets, debt tenures and factory reliability. Don't let this happen to you. Your first step is to understand what could go wrong, how likely it is to go wrong and what the consequences might be. This is usually done by systematic review at each of these three stages, making subjective estimates where necessary. For step one, what could go wrong, the classic approach is to inspect and audit activities for any clues. The audit has to be appropriate, the checking process has to be sufficiently frequent and comprehensive and those performing the audit have to have sufficient knowledge and experience. But the idea that potential failures can be detected through inspection is increasingly seen as only partially true. Although inspecting for failures is an obvious first step, it is not even close to being a hundred per cent reliable. Accumulated evidence from research and practical examples consistently indicate that most of us are not good at seeing what is in front of our noses.[xi] We need to retain audit and inspection, but see it as only one of a range of methods in preventing failure.

For stages two and three, assessing the likelihood of failure and its consequences, this is increasingly a formal exercise, even for subjective risks, that is carried out using standard frameworks. This approach is often prompted by health and safety concerns, environmental regulations and so on. You should record your major financial risks on this same framework, that is, keep all the risks in one place so that you can think about potential interactions among them. As you complete the framework, be aware of your own biases and don't assume that you are uniquely objective. Individual attitudes to risk, what we choose to pay attention to and how we take decisions, are complex. In fact many studies have demonstrated that people are generally poor at making risk-related judgements.[xii] Why else would we play the lottery, when the chances of getting killed in a car crash on the way to buy a ticket are much higher than the chance of winning the lottery itself? But, even if we don't always make rational decisions about the chances of failure, we can't abandon the attempt. Just be aware of the limits to your own rationality as you estimate failure and look at the issue from as many angles as possible to mitigate your own biases. This makes failure estimation a team sport.

Enhancing your risk identification radar

So the three stages are to review all possible risks, make an estimate of their probabilities and then assess the impact if the risk event happens. This work culminates in a risk matrix for your organization, summarized in Figure 5.3, by separating risks into four quadrants.

High probability risks might occur as frequently as once a year at one of your facilities, or at one of your finance operations, while low probability risks could occur as infrequently as once every ten years across global

FIGURE 5.3 Risk probability matrix

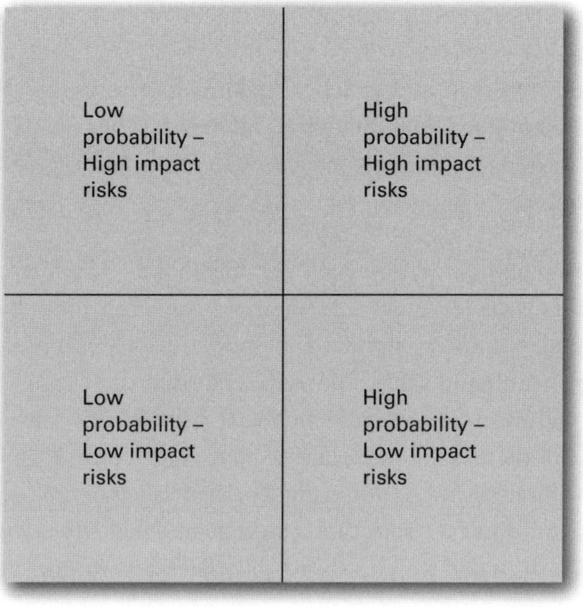

| Low probability – High impact risks | High probability – High impact risks |
| Low probability – Low impact risks | High probability – Low impact risks |

business generally. High impact risks are catastrophic, involving major human, environmental, financial, or brand and reputation damage that could destroy your firm. Low impact risks are recoverable incidents, like an unexpected 24-hour shutdown. We are not advocating that you use the matrix to multiply probability by outcome, but that you use it to get all the risks that need to be evaluated and planned for onto your radar. How you plan for prevention, mitigation and recovery will vary depending on the type of risk that you are dealing with.

Now let's look at your role in populating the risk matrix.

Finance leadership in building the risk matrix

Finance teams often do an outstanding job of managing their own risks, such as those arising from outsourcing finance functions, changes in expert staff, or tax or accounting policy and managing the sometimes creaky information systems that run your data. We have already made the case for you to include risks outside finance in your review. These might range from risks linked to ageing facilities (creeping risks); from changing external pressures on your host governments, suppliers and business partners (interdependency risks); and from new contractual arrangements, including mergers, acquisitions and divestments (intended and unintended risks).

Much of the data for identifying risk lies within the experience and judgement of your own organization, but it doesn't always make it across functional or business unit boundaries. So risk identification may be facilitated or led by finance, but it needs to be owned by the business and grounded in experienced business judgement. We support a bottom-up and top-down approach. It could well be that one of your units sees a risk before it is visible to the other units. For example, the treasury area may see the tightening of spreads, constriction of credit or days of accounts receivable increasing before the trend is observable to the business. Or, the logistics organization may observe falling container and shipping prices signalling an economic slowdown. As these two examples demonstrate, it may not be until individual or bottom-up risks are aggregated that the big picture emerges. Working simultaneously from bottom up and top down means that the company culture must support real-time learning and open communication. It won't work if people are afraid of being punished for not foreseeing risk initially. They need to be rewarded for sharing information that may provide other units with critical indicators.

Don't overlook the human element in risk

One of the easiest risks to miss is people risk. We tend to think of activities (new expenses' policy) and events (plant shutdown) but not necessarily people. How do you keep people risk on your radar? And while you may already have developed experience and judgement in many aspects of risk management, has your team, or the teams below them? Human risk is not just a question of lacking experts, or moving people around without the training to support them. It can be more serious.

Look at your team. Look at the executive team of your company, whether you are a member of it or not. One thing we know about leaders is that they find the tough people decisions the toughest. They can shut down operations, change business models, reinvent the strategy. But ask them to get rid of a dysfunctional team member and it's like drawing teeth (in the old-fashioned sense of pulling teeth out). They hum and haw and deliberate and take advice and, and, and.

Can you, as the objective CFO, have a voice here? So often, we have observed executive committees where there is a naughty member. Sometimes it's just harmless behaviour. Turning up late for meetings or not showing up at all. Telling jokes in the middle of a serious conversation. Being intermittently available for important decisions. Sometimes it's worse. They set member against member on the committee. They gossip where they shouldn't. They have a disruptive following within the organization. And sometimes it's immediately and obviously threatening to the reputation of the organization. They act but don't communicate to the rest of the team. They are mavericks. They break company policy on expenses. They have risky lifestyles. And yet, no one confronts them. In fact, often the opposite – the CEO, or team leader, may actively excuse their behaviour, or claim that it is under control and that the individual is vital to the team because of a specific expertise. Yet this is a potential high impact risk.

Much in organizational life is unpredictable and perhaps people most of all. When you see aberrant behaviour, call it. It adds the fourth dimension to Donald Rumsfeld's very clever categorization; it's an unknown known. We all see it, it's obvious, but it's subliminal, the outcome can't be predicted and no one speaks it out loud.

And look outside your organization

Most of your internally generated work will result in identifying high probability risks. To highlight others, including low-probability, high impact events that could have a significant impact, scan continuously outside your organization as well. This is where your external network kicks in again. This is far from a simple intellectual exercise and will test the limits of your intelligence gathering, analysis and business judgement. A few questions may help you:

- How well do you anticipate and monitor what is going on across your own industry and across business generally and which sources do you consult?

- What have you learned from so-called black swan events that have happened to others (and may actually have been predictable)?

- What processes do you use to concisely and rapidly communicate internally risks identified from external surveillance? Who needs to know?

- How do you maintain an internal environment of 'no surprises', to accelerate bad news reaching you?

Probability and impact – how bad could it really get?

Having identified your risks, you need to assess them for probability and impact, which is really saying that you need to understand your assumptions. Risk mitigation tools are helpless without human judgement. Human beings can ask the 'what if' questions that computer programs can't. What if the Middle East faces multiple wars across the region? How might the European Union fare if some of its member countries fail on their debt? What if sustained recession or corporate scandal brings increased regulation to burden business? What if there is a sudden reduction in China's growth or it stops buying treasuries and puts its significant capital into commodities? What if emerging markets drive 70 per cent of economic growth over the next 20 years? This is just a small sample of what should keep you up at night.

To heighten your risk awareness, consider the biases and assumptions that underlie your conclusions. For example, many firms manage within a standard borrowing ratio, to take advantage of the lower cost of debt relative to equity, while not taking on undue risk by over-borrowing. But the deep assumption is that you will never have the risk of not being able to borrow. In fact, most firms run on short-term credit, and in the event of a catastrophic event, the short-term lines of credit could be cut off and longer-term lenders could scrutinize their debt covenants for ways to accelerate repayment. What would you do if the money tap was cut off?

Mergers and acquisitions also expose you to a whole host of hidden risks. The largest risks, like long tail liabilities or adverse reputation, may be the very things that put the acquisition that you are targetting on the auction block in the first place. But if the target's risk management practices were lax enough to create the visible exposures, how robust are they likely to be in areas that are less visible? And how fast could you fix them?

You need to override the inherent optimism lower down in the organization. When someone says 'this can't happen because', you should hear alarm bells. Encourage them not to report only good news upwards, but to think in contingencies. As you go through your risk review, just as Bernard Katompa says, you may decide that you are better off exiting the line of business that is exposing you to the risk. Once it's on your radar, how do you try to prevent it happening?

Step 2: Risk prevention

Risk prevention is based on the idea that it is almost always better to avoid failures and their negative consequences than have to recover from them, which is why risk prevention is an important part of improving resilience. And the most obvious approach to risk prevention is to design out the possibility of things going wrong. This can be done by using the process mapping that was described in Chapter 3, or some variant of it. Start by identifying the activities or stages in the process that are particularly prone to failure and the stages that are critical to success, then they can be eliminated or made more robust. In effect, this is a process of simulation, where you metaphorically walk through the activities or processes, discussing each stage in turn and engineering out the potential risk points.

Failsafe mechanisms

A variant of engineering out risk is the use of failsafe mechanisms, which prevent the mistakes that can cause failure. This concept has emerged since the introduction of Japanese methods of operations' improvement. Called poka-yoke in Japanese,[xiii] it's based on the principle that human mistakes are inevitable. It's important to prevent them from creating risk. Poka-yokes are simple, preferably inexpensive, devices or systems that are incorporated into a process to prevent inadvertent mistakes resulting in a defect. Examples of simple failsafe mechanisms include using checklists which have to be completed in preparation for, or on completion of, an activity, or limiting the number of onscreen character fields to make it obvious when data has been mistyped. These basic approaches have been very effectively applied in a variety of situations from the cockpit of jumbo jets to operating theatres.

Redundant resources

Another option is to provide extra but redundant resources that can provide backup in the case of things going wrong. Having back-up resources can be an expensive solution to reduce the likelihood of the failure and is generally used when the failure could have a critical impact. Redundancy means doubling or even tripling some of the elements in a process so that these replacement elements can come into action when the principal element fails. We are used to the idea that hospitals and other public buildings have back-up electricity generators ready to operate in case the main electricity supply should fail. But the concept can be relevant in non-technical environments. For example, back-up staff may be held in reserve in case of unexpected demand or if key staff are prevented from working. Sports teams have back-ups for all the key positions to be ready for the unexpected but inevitable injury. In finance, think about the consultants and lawyers you keep on retainer – just in case.

Applying risk prevention for finance professionals

Douglas Flint, the Chairman of HSBC, takes an active role in building risk mitigation strategies regularly with his team:

> I give an exam question to my team. It might be something like, assume there's a material error in the accounts arising from a control weakness. Where do you think it is likely to have arisen? They write it down as individuals and then we compare answers. Often we all write down the same thing. Once we are all agreed, the next question is, well if we think that is where the risk lies, what are we going to do about it?

Finance leaders have a big responsibility for setting a good example when it comes to risk management. If it is on your agenda, as it is on Douglas', then the function will pay attention to it. Douglas doesn't just pay attention to it, he makes sure his team is aligned in planning for the worst case scenario.

In finance, risk prevention starts by paying attention to unrewarded risks. An unrewarded risk is like choosing not to wear a hard hat in a construction zone. How many unrewarded risks is your organization taking every day? You need to make process improvements to reduce or eliminate risk where taking the risk yields no competitive value for the firm. Examples in finance would be to stop taking undue foreign exchange risks and to think beyond accepting the lowest bid and instead hire contractors who meet your operational thresholds. It is important to make these unrewarded risks visible, because they often aren't, and address them quickly.

Again, take account of the human element in your risk prevention protocols. Data flow can be overwhelming, especially if people are working long hours and are tired. So try to simplify, with reports that automatically flag important indicators of risk. Chapter 2 covered how important good communication skills are to your success as a finance professional. Douglas Flint embellishes the point:

> 'You have to be more than analytical and move beyond reporting to interpreting. People will not pay attention or they will miss the point if it is buried in an overload of data. For example, you might want to flag an unexpectedly high level of overdue payments, or a rise in minor operational incidents above a long-standing baseline, then make it clear – don't expect people to work it out for themselves.'

You can also help to avoid human error through training in risk awareness, separating duties for critical activities and having an active, risk-minded internal audit function.

Layers of protection

If you can't eliminate a big risk, think about layering your failsafe mechanisms and redundant steps. Not all risks are equal, and so risk protection needs to be tailored to the level of risk you are considering. An obvious place for multiple layers of protection is for higher impact risks, because eventually one of the lines of defence will fail, either through human error or system or equipment failure. When you are shifting over to a major new system or process, or trying to consolidate a newly acquired business, or dealing with a crisis in one of your major partners, you will want extra layers of expertise and review to address quickly the known unknown. Use examples from other parts of the organization or from outside to make your case for this expenditure, because you will need buy-in from the wider organization.

As Douglas Flint reminded us in Chapter 1, spending on finance is often counter cyclical, because you need it most when times are toughest. And risk prevention isn't nearly as exciting as swooping in and putting out the fire after an emergency, when you have the opportunity to look like a hero as you save the day. But imagine if they had relocated the power generators at Fukushima to higher ground and prevented the flooding that led to the eventual melt-down? That's the kind of case you will need to make.

For more serious risks, work to create alignment with the businesses on prioritized steps for deploying risk protection and adopt performance management tools, such as metrics and milestones, to ensure these steps are actually deployed on schedule. Make sure your audit programme is focused on testing the robustness of the protection you do have in place. And, again, think about the hidden risk exposure you face through third parties such as contractors and encourage them to think about their own risk prevention practices.

Barnacles can clog the ship and stop her moving

Layers of protection are relevant and often brought in after a particular setback. But over time, these fixes can pile up like barnacles. We rarely step back to examine how these fixes interrelate, to judge whether they still provide effective layers of protection, or just false confidence. And if these redundant, protective layers have been added by different people at different times, they may even increase your risk profile. They can countermand each other, misdirect effort or simply bog you down in red tape. That's when risk prevention gets a bad name. Ask your auditors to keep a log of setbacks as a checklist for examining how your risk management system has been constructed and is functioning in practice.

Periodic review

Fortunately, you are not starting from scratch. Once your risk prevention practices are in place, you can focus your energy on looking for the edge where continuous improvement in risk protection is needed. Think about putting a regular rotation of risk protection processes on a watch list for review, to make it easier to focus more deeply on a particular area of risk. You may identify something of unforeseen significance, or you may decide that you are over-investing in a certain area of risk protection and can scale back and save money without undue increase in risk.

You also need to examine your underlying assumptions regarding the resilience of your prevention and mitigation plans and take a more fundamental look at your actual worst case risk exposure if your plans fail. We can't prevent everything, bad things do happen, systems and processes deteriorate over time, smallish risks accumulate and when they reach a critical point you need to be sure about what you think will happen, not what you hope will happen.

Step 3: Risk mitigation

And then, one day, it does happen. Somewhat sadly, you will only be able to celebrate the wisdom of all this planning when something, predictably, goes wrong. Not a time when you'll feel like celebrating. How do we reduce the effect of things going wrong?

Risk mitigation means isolating a failure from its negative consequences. It can involve a number of mitigation actions. And while the action taken will vary depending on the exact nature of the risk, there are some generic categories that give a flavour of the types of mitigation that are generally useful.

Economic mitigation

This includes actions such as insurance against losses, spreading the financial consequences of failure and hedging against failure (what Bernard Katompa earlier called transferring risk to a third party). Insurance is the best known of these and is widely adopted. Spreading the financial consequences of failure could involve, for example, spreading contracts among supply companies to reduce the financial consequences of such companies failing. Hedging involves creating a portfolio of ventures whose outcomes are not correlated, so as to reduce total variability. This often takes the form of financial instruments, for example, a business may purchase a financial hedge against the price risk of a vital raw material deviating significantly from a set price.

Spatial containment

This means stopping the failure physically spreading to affect other parts of an internal or external supply network. Preventing misleading data from being transmitted to partners, for example, could depend on predictive algorithms used to spot data anomalies. Similarly ring-fencing accounts so a deficit in one account cannot be made good from another account could contain the effects of account fraud.

Temporal containment

This means containing the spread of a failure over time. It particularly applies when information about a failure or potential failure needs to be transmitted without delay. In the case of account theft, investing in software that detects signs of possible unusual account behaviour is an example of temporal containment.

Loss reduction

This covers any action that reduces the catastrophic consequences of failure by removing the resources that are likely to suffer those consequences. For example, building in transfer delays until approval for major withdrawals has been given to mitigate against fraud.

Substitution

This means compensating for failure by providing other resources that can substitute for those rendered less effective by the failure. It is a little like the concept of redundancy that was described earlier, but does not always imply excess resources if a failure has not occurred. For example, ensuring that reserve funds and staff to manage the transfer can be speedily brought into play can reduce the impact of account fraud. Another example is keeping track of your finance team members' key crisis management skills , including bringing back recent retirees, so that they can be quickly deployed from their regular jobs if they are needed in an emergency.

Be ready

No one ever really expects their risk prevention systems to fail. What makes you a custodian of value is that you are realistic and know that one day your risk prevention will fail somewhere and you will need to mitigate the consequences. How resilient are your contingency plans for the risks on your risk matrix compared to the examples above? Do you have adequate insurance to mitigate the financial consequences of the loss? How will you stop the contagion from spreading, as governments, customers and suppliers react? How will you avoid sustained erosion in stakeholder confidence? How will you protect other assets from falling prey to the incident, such as seizure by nervous creditors? And when the incident affects your ability to meet customer requirements, how will you find alternative sources of supply?

We tend to stop with relatively simple mitigation steps. For risks with smaller consequences this may be acceptable, but not for your major risks. Risk management means thinking seriously about what you, your finance team and your organization must do to mitigate risk when it does arise. Being prepared will also give you and your team greater confidence to adopt creative solutions quickly to confront the situations you will face.

For example, if there is a major systems failure at one of your outsourced service providers, you will need to find ways to close the books and pay your invoices, or concern about you will spread quickly. If you have an inadvertent lapse in regulatory compliance, or alternatively, a misapplication of the rules by the regulator, you need to know your regulators well enough to deal with the issue constructively, or a small event could escalate. If a major business partner is either unable or unwilling to continue funding a venture, you will want a back-up plan to avoid being forced to sell the business. And if a major new deal, on which your business plans are based, is blocked by lawsuits and other delays in regulatory approval, you will need to keep the rest of the business on track and producing revenue while you deal with the setback.

Testing and living your mitigation plans

Most organizations have emergency response plans. Keep them relevant and alive by testing them in live scenarios with practical exercises. Do your people know what they should do and who is responsible for which activity? It is good if the exercise adds some new twists along the way, additional complications that might not have occurred to people. The exercise might start with the default of a major supplier; become compounded by rumours that your firm is going to default on contractual delivery obligations; be accelerated by an over-tightening of lines of credit and sudden shareholder worry about the firm's long-term future; and hit a crescendo with a fire at one of your major facilities. Don't try to replicate a real incident, because reality never plays out precisely as predicted in the planning exercise. Instead, use these contingency planning exercises to strengthen individuals' mindsets about risk mitigation. Keep them alive to the possibilities and alert to the interdependencies between separate failures.

Overreact

If an incident really happens, this is no time to exercise your usual objective restraint. Overreact. In other words, once you know your layers of protection have been breached, mobilize everything you have in the first hours of the response. You can always stand down surplus resources later. But it may well turn out that the application of superior force was the saving decision in bringing the crisis to a quick and early halt. Let's take two examples.

During the summer of 2011, hurricane Irene was predicted to hit New York City. Knowing that it would take more than 24 hours for the city to mobilize a comprehensive response, the city leadership made the tough call to execute their contingency plan. This included shutting down mass transportation, evacuating hundreds of thousands of people and getting property out of harm's way. By the time it hit New York, the hurricane had become a relatively minor storm. So should they have evacuated? There has been a lot of debate and that's where judgement comes in. The city leadership decided to avoid the extensive human suffering that might have occurred. You could face similar criticism for evasive action and need to be ready with a well thought through reason for your response to a potential risk. Of course, the lack of pre-emptive action by the US government, to the threat and aftermath of hurricane Katrina in 2005, has been similarly criticized. New Orleans was devastated, nearly 1,500 lives were lost and there was billions of dollars of damage from which the city has still not recovered.

Keep everyone informed

Tell the significant people involved what you are proposing to do about the failure. It is critical that you don't just get on with fixing things. People have to know. In service operations this is especially important where customers need to be kept informed, both for their peace of mind and to demonstrate that something is being done. In all operations, however, it is important to communicate what action is going to happen so that everyone can set their own plans in motion. And make sure that your mitigation efforts really have contained the failure, in order to stop the consequences spreading and causing further failures. The precise containment actions will depend on the nature of the failure. Finally, there needs to be some kind of follow-up to make sure that the containment actions really have permanently stopped the problem.

The actual work of mitigating a risk event is hard, stressful and yet surprisingly exhilarating. It is hard because you just need to grit your teeth and grind through it, as it's not just going to go away. Stressful – because you don't really know how bad it is going to get, how long it will last and if ultimately you are going to be successful. And it's exhilarating because often the chaos brings out the best in real leaders who take charge, make the tough decisions and see them through. After the immediate crisis passes, people often recall the greater autonomy and visible results they were able to enjoy, compared to their normal day-to-day responsibilities. A crisis well handled pulls people together and raises morale. That's why it's worth practising.

Now let's turn to our final step of recovering from the fallout after a risk has materialized.

Step 4: Risk recovery

Once the initial incident is finally over – and sooner or later it will be – you need to take steps to help your organization recover and to learn from what went wrong.

All types of operation can benefit from well-planned recovery, partly because it shapes people's perceptions of failure. Even where customers, for example, see a failure, it may not necessarily lead to dissatisfaction. People accept that things occasionally do go wrong. It is not necessarily the failure itself that leads to dissatisfaction but often the organization's response to it. It's how you deal with it. Recovering well from a public failure can even enhance a business's reputation.[xiv]

Risk recovery as an opportunity

Downside risk brings both the opportunity to show who you really are as a leader in the face of adversity, as well as the opportunity to learn and further strengthen your risk management mindset. Recovery and learning from an incident will help your organization shift from a prescriptive command, control and compliance approach to risk towards a mindset of co-creating an evergreen risk management process.

Once the initial incident is contained, it is tempting to declare victory, congratulate all involved and take a break to recover from the long days of stress. That is precisely the wrong thing to do. Even if it's safely behind you, you need to determine what actually happened, and why, to avoid a repetition. There is also the work of recovering your reputation and rebuilding relationships to minimize the long-term impact of the incident. All of your stakeholders will have seen you respond to the incident and they are likely to be pondering the deeper implications of the risk event. If you can tell them what happened, and if you keep them informed about your recovery plans, you may be able to retain confidence in your organization's ability to exercise good judgement and to be a good corporate citizen. If you don't, the incident may raise unfortunate and deeper concerns among stakeholders.

Learning from failure

The time just after the incident is the ideal time to capture what you have learned from it – about your ability to foresee risk, the strength of your prevention systems, the capacity of your mitigation processes and the relevance of your training and leadership development programmes. Learning from your own risk events is very important. It shouldn't be a witch hunt to punish the guilty, but an investigation to get to the bottom of why the risk was inadequately identified, assessed, managed, or mitigated.

Failure helps us to learn. In failure planning, learning involves revisiting the failure to find out its root cause and then engineering out the causes of the failure so that it will not happen again. Learning the lessons from a failure is not the end of it. Unless we formally incorporate the lessons into plans for reacting to future failures we will not really have learnt much and will have failed to improve. This is real activity that loops us back to our risk prevention activities in Step 2. If the incident is severe enough, the learnings may be so substantial that you will not simply revert back to your pre-existing risk matrices, layers of protection and contingencies. Instead you are more likely to use what you have learned to raise your risk management game. Once our new risk prevention steps are in place, we then loop back to Step 1, risk identification, to work through in theory how the reconstituted system might react to failures in the future. Once again, this involves identifying all the possible failures which might occur and then formally defining the procedures which the organization should follow for each type of failure identified.

Continuously improving your risk management processes

We've now taken you through the entire risk management cycle – identification, prevention, mitigation and recovery and learning. We hope you have identified areas that are already working well within your organization and also spotted some potential gaps that need investigation. In fact, if you have seen gaps, then you are already demonstrating a risk management mindset. The thread that binds it all together is the fundamental philosophy of continuous improvement of processes. And luckily, leaders like you are never satisfied, you are always looking for a better way to do things.

In that spirit, ask yourself some questions:

- How well am I monitoring my risk identification processes to ensure that they are functioning as intended?
- What sort of improvement plans do we have in place for prevention and mitigation of our larger risks and are these improvement plans on track and properly resourced?
- What sort of assurance programme do we have to determine how well the risk management mindset is being deployed deeper in the organization and are the findings being acted upon?

Sustaining continuous improvement in risk management across the enterprise is a major undertaking. We think you should dedicate some full-time risk management resources to the task. These risk process managers can help ensure that the firm's approach to risk management is consistently applied, streamlined and that all the various pieces fit together well. They will need to consolidate a multitude of risk data from a wide variety of sources of differing content and quality and prepare meaningful and incisive analysis that shows trends. They can help facilitate thoughtful conversation and cumulative learning in the executive committee. It will take some upfront investment, but this will show a good return once the protocols are developed.

Summary ... and looking ahead

We have made the case for you to take a broad role in risk management in addition to looking out for your risks in finance. That's because every risk, wherever it is in the business, has an impact on your numbers. In the end, the CFO needs to ensure that the top leadership team is focused on balancing all risk, whether financial, legal, operational, safety, environmental, security, political, supply chain or human resources. Reinforcing core risk management skills with process and leadership excellence will make you a more powerful and a more effective player.

A risk management mindset will prepare you to ask and help answer some of the more strategic risk questions that will have an impact on value creation. Questions like whether a disruptive business model is about to transform your industry? Or how you balance the dilemma of making space for entrepreneurs and innovative business models while continuing to drive performance of the existing business today? Or whether poor succession planning is putting the enterprise in jeopardy?

By deploying the risk management tools we've outlined in this chapter[xv] and sustaining the robust control environment described in Chapter 4, you are well on your way to securing or validating your place on the executive team.

Chapter 6 – Investment

So far we have covered the finance function's role in Control and Risk and how these activities underpin value, largely through preventing loss. The final piece in the puzzle is how finance can help the organization to make sound investments to build the business. Investments are an outlay of capital today for a benefit tomorrow. They might be investments in improving processes, in improving products, or, as with an M&A transaction, they can be both. While most of us readily agree on the importance of investing in the business, some may be less aware of the need to invest in finance itself. We see finance as a business within a business. As business owners, we need to focus on meeting our budgets and also on whether we have the right resources deployed. We should focus on the additional value that could be created by investing in finance and not just on continuing to execute our regular daily activities.

What do we think about when we try to increase the value add of the finance function? Yes, that's right, cost reduction. We agree that active cost management is an important contributor to value creation for finance and for the firm. But cost management needs to be done strategically, the very antithesis of the slash and burn approach we often see. Finance needs to demonstrate actively the value we bring to the entire enterprise through value protection and creation. Our fundamental value protection services of control and risk management sustain value by avoiding loss. Our value creation services typically include evaluation and execution of investment decisions and corporate transactions. We are pretty good at calculating expected value. It's quite a different matter for finance to take a role in ensuring that the expected value is actually delivered. Yet we can support this through continuous improvement, competitive benchmarking and periodically adjusting our finance service offerings.

You could write a book on how best to deliver value through investments. Our goal is to be slightly less ambitious. In Chapter 6, we will provide some core insights into the investment mindset. We will cover how, as a finance professional, you need to think about your service portfolio, how to manage your cost profile, how to understand your revenue stream and how you convey the importance of all of this to your extended finance team and to the business.

Notes

[i] The DNA of the CFO, E&Y 2010.

[ii] Webster's New International Dictionary, 1935, Second Edition Unabridged.

[iii] The Fukushima Daiichi nuclear disaster is a series of equipment failures, nuclear meltdowns, and releases of radioactive materials at the Fukushima I Nuclear Power Plant, following the Tōhoku earthquake and tsunami on 11 March 2011. The Fukushima disaster is the largest nuclear accident since the 1986 Chernobyl disaster, but it is more complex as multiple reactors and spent fuel pools are involved. At the time of the earthquake, Reactor 4 had been de-fuelled while 5 and 6 were in cold shutdown for planned maintenance. The remaining reactors shut down automatically after the earthquake, with emergency generators starting up to run the control electronics and water pumps needed to cool reactors. The entire plant was flooded by the 15 m tsunami wave, including low-lying generators and electrical switchgear in reactor basements and external pumps for supplying cooling seawater. The connection to the electrical grid was broken as the tsunami destroyed the power lines. All power for cooling was lost and reactors started to overheat. The flooding and earthquake damage hindered external assistance.

[iv] Allister Wilson is a partner at Ernst & Young. We also quoted him in Chapters 1, 2 and 4.

[v] Nassim Nicholas Taleb wrote the book The Black Swan in 2007. Taleb believes that many major events (like the internet and First World War) are like black swans, undirected and unpredicted. The black swan was presumed not to exist and was not documented in the west until the eighteenth century.

[vi] The Perfect Storm is a 2000 disaster film directed by Wolfgang Petersen. It is an adaptation of the 1997 non-fiction book of the same title by Sebastian Junger

about the crew of the *Andrea Gail* that got caught in the Perfect Storm of 1991 – two powerful weather fronts and a hurricane.

vii 'Risk Management 2.0: Reassessing Risk in an Interconnected World', interview with Erwann Michel-Kerjan Wharton, by Karen Christensen, Rotman Magazine Fall 2010, University of Toronto.

viii See Chapter 2 for notes on the Arab Spring.

ix Peter Sellers was hilarious as the bumbling French inspector in this series of films. One storyline was about his relationship with Cato, his house boy, an expert in martial arts. It's never clear whether Cato thinks Clouseau is a great detective or whether he humours him. It is a running joke that he is instructed to unexpectedly attack the inspector, to keep Clouseau's combat skills and vigilance sharp. Always alert. Just like a CFO and risk.

x 'There are known knowns; there are things we know we know. We also know there are known unknowns; that is to say we know there are some things we do not know. But there are also unknown unknowns – the ones we don't know we don't know.' Former US Secretary of Defense, Donald Rumsfeld, 12 February 2002, at a press briefing talking about absence of evidence linking the government of Iraq with the supply of weapons of mass destruction to terrorist groups.

xi If you haven't seen the invisible gorilla movie, look at this link or look it up on YouTube. Observers are asked to count the number of times the white team passes a ball in a warm-up for basketball. While they are playing someone dressed in a gorilla costume walks across the screen and waves. Most observers can give a number for the basketball moves but fail to see the gorilla at all. **www.livescience.com/6727-invisible-gorilla-test-shows-notice.html**. For a more academic take on the subject, review Mark Becker; Harold Pashler (Dec 2002), 'Volatile visual representations: failing to detect changes in recently processed information', *Psychonomic Bulletin and Review* 9(4): 744–750 and related literature.

xii We don't have the space to do justice to this fascinating topic in this book. You could start with Jonah Lehrer How We Decide, Houghton Mifflin Harcourt 2009, which shows that decisions are based on split second emotional reactions that we then post-hoc justify with fact. Even the emotion we feel at the time has an impact on our judgement; anger makes us more optimistic, fear makes us more pessimistic. Cognition and Emotion Volume 14 Issue 4 2000, pages 473–493, 'Beyond valence: Toward a model of emotion-specific influences on judgement and choice', J.S. Lerner and D. Keltner.

xiii From yokeru (to prevent) and poka (inadvertent errors).

xiv Johnson and Johnson are renowned for the way in which they responded to the Chicago disaster in 1982, when seven people died after taking pain-relief Tylenol capsules that had been poisoned through an unknown person lacing them in the shops with potassium cyanide. They halted all Tylenol production and advertising, issued a nationwide recall of all Tylenol products (some 31 million bottles) and offered a $100,000 reward. The killer was never found.

[xv] This chapter has drawn on material from the interim report of the National Academies Effectiveness of Safety and Environmental Management Systems for outer Continental Shelf Oil and Gas Operations 21 June 2011; and from Precursor Analysis for Offshore Oil and Gas Drilling – from Prescriptive to Risk-Informed Regulation by Roger M. Cooke, Heather L. Ross and Adam Stern, Resources for the Future, (NGO), January 2011.

Growing value through investment

We have covered how control and risk management stop value leaking out of the organization, as well as gaining value through making you more efficient and effective. But the biggest lever you have at your disposal for creating value is definitely through investment. The trick is not to get so bogged down in your daily activities that you miss the opportunity to play in this space. Your licence to operate comes from tight management of risk and control. It's what gets you a seat at the table. And once you are at the table, as Douglas Flint, the Chairman of HSBC puts it – this is the fun part.

CASE STUDY Don't get bogged down in the daily grind

Gordon was thinking seriously about retiring in about two years. So when he approached this year's succession planning review with the executive team, he paid extra attention to honing his arguments about who was fit to succeed him. Of his multiple direct reports, he saw three as being ready now to take over from him. But when the time came to put his case, he only got as far as citing their names before his CEO interrupted: 'Gordon, I'm not so sure about these candidates. They are all good people and decent at their current jobs. But I don't think they see the big picture well enough to take over from you. Our new CFO should be somebody who can help us build value, not someone who just covers the fundamentals.'

The CEO continued: 'For example, your treasurer Mark seems to have had a pretty choppy delivery last year, and on top of that, he went 7 per cent over budget. I need a CFO with a stronger operational focus.' These words stung Gordon, because Mark had actually performed heroically last year in dealing with a huge refinancing problem caused by weaknesses in their core banks. And while he did need to bring in external help to fight the crisis, Mark and his team had worked extensive overtime to keep the overruns to an absolute minimum. Gordon now regretted his decision to shield the executive team from the challenges Mark had faced.

At this point, the new head of HR chimed in. 'Sally, your head of accounting, is fine as far as she goes, but based on my personal experience from outside this industry, backed up by benchmarking data I've just received, it is obvious that Accounting has excess headcount, and Sally is doing nothing about it.' Gordon winced, because he had talked to Sally about managing her headcount to a lower level, but had not made it a priority in light of all of the other changes she was facing due to new reporting regulations. But he should have seen this one coming. The new HR head was bound to bring in her own ideas and Mark hated being caught out in a drive-by benchmarking. The data were probably accurate in theory, but took no account of local circumstances.

Not to be outdone, the COO added, 'There must be something wrong with Karen, your head of management information. She forecast that each of our approved investment propositions would add to shareholder value and yet our aggregate return on capital continues to drift downwards year after year.' Gordon had to bite his lip on this one, because in reality Karen was under-staffed. Her team barely had the resources to run the input numbers through the economic models and no time for real analysis before their work was turned into management presentations. And to add insult to injury, the numbers and critical assumptions themselves came from the COO's own unit.

Gordon tried. 'You know, I think this is my fault. I have probably concentrated too hard on doing the job and making sure you get the data you need, when you want it. If I had let you peek inside the black box you would have seen how much we have been struggling with some of the challenges we have been facing. Judging Mark, Sally and Karen on their performance based on inadequate resources isn't a fair test of their capabilities.' This didn't get much of a reaction. After a short gap in the conversation, Gordon's CEO suggested three new names as potential CFO candidates. 'These are very strong people from the line organization', the CEO said. 'There is no question that they really understand the concept of growing shareholder value. They are all outstanding leaders and what they may lack in finance expertise can be compensated for by the subject matter experts on your existing team. Give it some thought, Gordon.'

Does it matter?

Why shouldn't someone from the line take over as CFO? After all, the majority of CEOs in Europe[i] and elsewhere come from the finance function, so there is plenty of movement in the opposite direction. What matters is that the role is filled by the best candidate who will do most to support the enterprise. Gordon's challenge is that he believes he does have the best candidate, in fact three of them, from within the finance function. The problem is that he hasn't sold them to the executive team. Each of his candidates is seen to be underperforming at the finance fundamentals, because Gordon has hidden the real challenges they are facing in executing with inadequate resources. Worse, he is complicit in their failure. By not making the case for more investment in the finance function, as part of a positive growth strategy for the organization, he has allowed them to be seen to be failing at the fundamentals. He has inadvertently taken away their licence to operate. And currently, they are not seen as good enough to sit at the table.

In this chapter we cover investment, both what it is and some of the obstacles we face in pursuing it. Then we look at moving beyond our limitations to really investing in finance, as a function, so that it is seen as a credible part of value creation and not just an overhead function. We zero in on the topic of cost control, looking at techniques like benchmarking and continuous improvement to help us reduce costs in our function and across the business. Finally, we look at the specific role that finance can play in value creation through taking a strategic role in the organization's investment strategy, including your role at the negotiating table. Let's start with our definition of investment.

Defining investment

Our trusty 1935 edition of Webster's defines investment as: 'The investing of money or capital in some species of property for income or profit'. Wikipedia offers:

> In Finance, Investment is putting money into something with the expectation of gain, that upon thorough analysis, has a high degree of security for the principal amount, as well as security of return, within an expected period of time. In contrast putting money into something with an expectation of gain without thorough analysis, without security of principal, and without security of return is speculation or gambling.

If you see your role as CFO to speculate or gamble, we are all in trouble. Naturally, we will be examining how you add value through sound investment. So, we won't be covering stock market trading or similar activities. In this chapter, we will confine our discussion to investments that help grow enterprise value. Nor will we be covering basic investment analysis tools and techniques like NPV, IRR,[ii] sensitivity analysis, scenario analysis and so on. We will focus on a robust review of creating value from investments, as well as how to identify and articulate the value that you and your finance organization deliver. These are your twin strategic tasks. As our story above illustrates, Gordon has a personal reputation for being good at creating value from investments and is credited with seeing the big picture. What he has failed to do is to demonstrate the value that the finance function is delivering. As in earlier chapters, before we look at what you should be doing, we will pause to think about some of the obstacles that you may need to overcome before you start.

Issues finance needs to confront

Your aim is to be a force for good in helping your enterprise to grow through investment. There are two barriers that may stand in your way. The first is that finance may be seen as an overhead, only there to support the line business, rather than as a strategic investment for the organization, with its own clear functional investment strategy. The second is that you may lack the credibility to be influential with the line business, at the executive level or elsewhere. Obviously these two are linked. As we have said before, your credibility rests in delivering the fundamentals to the business – reliable data that enables executives to take timely decisions. Let's start with how you are seen.

How are you seen by the business?

Enterprise value is an outcome measure. Like the football league tables, it's an aggregation of your organization's many wins and losses, plus a projection of your fitness for the longer term, assessed against the competition. The same model holds true for assessing how finance contributes value to the enterprise. Your business executives will note finance's successes as well as your setbacks and will gauge whether your team is alert and disciplined, or tired and overweight. Even more fundamentally, they will judge whether finance really is out there on the pitch with them as a true business partner, tackling the competition and working with operations as an important player on the enterprise team – or just playing a more peripheral or compliance oriented role. Let's explore a few images they might have of you.

Umpire, reporter, groundskeeper or cheerleader?

Do they see you as an umpire, enforcing the rules? An important part of your job is to ensure financial discipline across the firm, but if that's all they see you doing, you are in trouble. We all see the need for police, but it's not much fun constantly being pulled over or spot checked, particularly if we're not doing anything wrong. As Mohit Bhatia, the CFO of Genpact, puts it: 'I have multiple roles as business partner, strategic planner, investor relations and so on. I am both Super Cop and Chief Service Provider to my internal customers.' Super cop is only part of the story.

Maybe they see you as a reporter, telling the story? Finance prepares and issues the quarterly and annual financial reports, ensuring that these reports are accurate, transparent and presented in an understandable way. The figures need to be objective and fair. But you are not your figures. Try to avoid being so independently-minded that you create the impression that you have no personal stake. The story you are telling is not about someone else or simply a historical view of what has been achieved or missed. You are on the field playing as well as reporting from the sidelines. Rather than simply reporting the facts, sports teams keep their own statistics to improve the performance of their team – finance must have the same mindset.

Or perhaps they see you as a groundskeeper, silently hitting your numbers? Many fundamental finance tasks are like keeping the weeds down, not overly heroic, but someone needs to do it. But while many finance professionals like to be left alone provided they stay on budget, simply running silently in the background is not enough. If running silently is sufficient for you, then the function is likely to be seen as a necessary but burdensome cost centre, with every opportunity taken to cut the overhead. And of course, you should exploit outsourcing and other opportunities to stay lean and effective. What you don't want is an unthinking edict to cut costs by 10 per cent or so across the board. While keeping your own financial house in order, you should be explicit that you are doing just that – it's in order – and also vocal about the value that finance adds to the enterprise.

Another possible view of finance could be as cheerleader for investments and deals. Running the numbers in support of executive proposals is important, because there usually are more ideas for investing money than there is money to invest, so your role in helping prioritize among options is critical. But are you able to stand back from the numbers and have your own objective view? Do you have the confidence to recommend against pursuing an investment despite it being a senior executive's passion? In fact, balancing the dilemma of being at times a cheerleader and at other times, a dementor.[iii]

Your aim is to be seen as a real partner of the business and co-creator of value. Mohit Bhatia again:

> To be effective and get things done, you need credibility and respect equity, as opposed to a designation or title. They must respect your judgement and know that you are looking out for the best for the organization. You achieve this by having a healthy rapport with others and by being a good communicator.

We have dealt with some of the obstacles that you may face in becoming a guiding voice in the investment debate. Now let's think about the investment itself, both investing in the finance function and investing in the business.

The finance investment strategy

How do you move beyond being seen as a fixed overhead to being seen as a strategic investment for the organization, with your own functional investment strategy? It's not enough to talk about creating value, it's how you translate those words into a value creation mindset, for yourself and for your function. More than anything, it's about what you do and what you are seen to do. And an easy way to demonstrate a value creation mindset is to run your own function like a business.

There is a range of opportunities to create value by making investments within finance, which can establish an important track record of credibility with the line. Are you doing this? Even if you don't run the whole of finance, are you doing it for the unit that you do lead? If you don't develop your own strategy, you may be handed one. Cost management is one of your big strategic value levers. How proactive are you in addressing your cost effectiveness, both in terms of absolute costs as well as in terms of performance against external benchmarks? Is your finance function fit, fat, or anorexic? How do you know? Is your cost structure and talent pool sustainable for the longer term? You can't afford to take a passive or careless approach to costs if you are to be seen as a custodian of value. And starting with your own costs gives you a more credible voice when you scrutinize and criticize others' costs.

Bernard Katompa, CEO of Liberty Africa, has an interesting take on shifting your mindset on costs:

> Traditionally we think about fixed and variable costs. I think we should regard all costs as variable. Fixed costs may be fixed at the total level, but they can still vary at the unit level. So if you can improve performance and productivity, you can reduce costs at the unit level and by doing so, enhance the bottom line.

Here's a CFO who will leave no stone unturned in his quest for efficiency.

In the same way, you should be doing your own benchmarking, so you know how efficient you are compared with others, inside and outside your industry. Otherwise, like Gordon, you will be subjected to someone else's view of how well you stack up. There is plenty of external competition from financial consultants and outsourcing firms, who in effect compete with you and your finance team for management attention, budget and ultimately finance market share.

How valuable is the finance function?

How do you help others to see the value that finance brings to the enterprise? The defensive activities that we have already covered, like providing a robust control environment, risk management programmes and ensuring low-cost and flexible access to capital, are critical to your reputation. They can also be taken for granted unless you take the time to explain to your stakeholders what these activities contribute to shareholder value. If anything, the value of offensive activities, like your contribution in ensuring that new investments and M&A deals deliver value, is even harder to measure and get credit for. It still has to be done.

Run it like your own business

Think about it like running your own consultancy. Like any good business person, you need to take time periodically to examine the quality and mix of your service offerings. Don't perpetuate the status quo, but look to maintain your edge in value-orientation. Review your portfolio and understand how your product lines compare to the competition. Do your internal customers really value your products and services? Are you making a profit on your current product lines? With such a busy day job, we suspect that many of you are not asking yourselves enough of these questions or proactively measuring and articulating the value you contribute.

You don't have complete freedom of manouevre. Obviously you are not going to withdraw from providing critical services like tax to the firm, but you could look inside the portfolio of services your tax department is providing. Examine each of the finance departments in the same way. Armed with insights on cost performance and value for each of these services, you can plot them on a matrix such as the one shown in Figure 6.1.

FIGURE 6.1 Managing your business portfolio

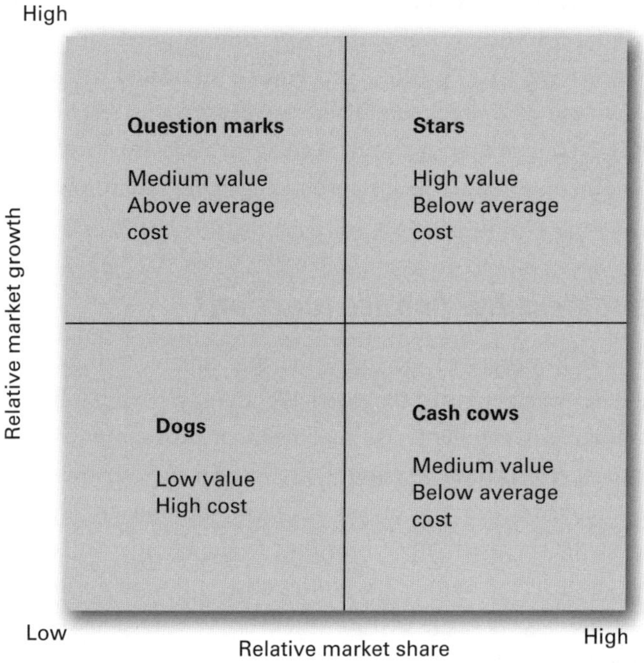

High

	Question marks	Stars
	Medium value	High value
	Above average	Below average
	cost	cost

Relative market growth

	Dogs	Cash cows
		Medium value
	Low value	Below average
	High cost	cost

Low   High

Relative market share

Yes, we know this matrix[iv] has been around for ages. And in its original, mathematical format, it wasn't so user-friendly. But at a high level, it will work to start a really good strategic discussion about your finance portfolio and what you should keep and what you might drop. As you apply the matrix, you are looking for high value services, in the eyes of your customers, and how to improve the most valuable ones. You can also overlay the analysis from one area, like tax, on top of another, like M&A, to build a complete picture.

It's the language that makes this such a great tool. Finance services that are high value and below average cost are your stars. They will probably be important to the business strategy (a differentiator) as well as important to the finance strategy. You should invest in them and decide if other services could be added or brought in-house. Using M&A as an example, you may wish to build internal capability for standard transactions, to reduce the cost of retainers and success fees. Alternatively, a well chosen third party service might add further value. Pay attention to maintaining your stars, as they typically attract cost over time and lose some of their shine.

Low-value, high-cost services are your dogs. They probably don't differentiate the business or support the efficiency of the finance function. A dog is a prime candidate for outsourcing, but you should also look closely at why you even provide such a service. Has it been running on auto-pilot for years, set up initially to address a business problem or request that is no longer relevant? You could try to rescue a dog by reducing costs, but given the low value it brings, is it really worth it? Will the business miss this service, if you can persuade them to give it up? If your dog is a statutory duty, you will need to get your costs down or outsource it.

In between are your medium value services. Those with good cost bench-marks are cash cows, which should be sustained and literally milked for their value. Well run service centres often fit the cash cow definition. Cash cows also need monitoring, because they can deteriorate too. If they are not managed properly they can lose value, attract costs and become dogs. Those with above average costs are your question marks. Turning these services into cash cows by reducing cost is one good option. They may have hidden value potential and you might be able to turn them into stars by recruiting some internal experts, or adding expertise from third parties who have built capability. One way or another, you need to take charge of your question marks, because they also have a habit of becoming dogs.

It will take time to work out where your services fit on the value–cost matrix, but it will pay dividends. And include your extended team in the discussion, so that everyone gets the idea about looking at the value that finance brings. As you proactively manage your portfolio, you will be demonstrating to the executive team also how serious you are about value creation.

Marketing

How much attention are you paying to telling your own story, marketing your services to retain and expand your customer base? If the line can see your role in value creation, your influence will grow. But marketing is rarely an area of strength for you. The pitch sometimes sounds like this: 'We acknowledge that it is difficult to value finance's efforts. However, we do good work, we have minimal errors or missed deadlines and anyone who knows business would have to be impressed.' Some try a more analytical approach: 'We processed 1.2 million data inputs from 124 locations across the globe, with an extended team of 8459 FTEs, and were able to close the books at our stretch target of 14 work days.' Makes sense in your world, but maybe not in theirs.

Admittedly these examples are caricatures. Yet think about the sales pitch for a car. Does the car dealer say, 'Trust me, this car is fine.'? Not likely. Instead, he talks to you, finds out a bit about you and pretty soon is honing in on the three to four things that all say 'this car was made for you'. The three to four factors of importance will vary by customer – a young family, a 22 year old with her first job and a 55 year old executive will each have different requirements. The experienced salesperson will zoom in on what it takes to sell a car to each of them.

So do you know the three to four things that are most important to each of your customers – your CEO, the other line executives, the other service organizations? How well are you delivering against their respective priorities? Do you share how your performance stacks up against best in class benchmarks and enrol them in your improvement plans? We are not advocating a slick marketing campaign, which you would hate and so would the executives on the receiving end. And don't ask them to fill out surveys, giving the impression that you really don't know much at all. This is simply about being clear about what you do and why you are good at it. If you don't tell them, how else will they know?

Communicate, communicate, communicate

As we said in Chapter 3, one of the striking things about meeting Mohit Bhatia is how quickly he can communicate with numbers. He interprets the data and then hands it to you in a way that has immediate meaning. He knows exactly how his finance function measures up:

> Finance is not the best on cost in our industry, we are on the median. We are a high growth company and need to reduce our number of legacy systems to get our costs down. As far as the business goes, there are areas where we delight them and places where we need to play catch up. I know what they are and we are working on them and they know that. It's a journey of continuous

improvement. I need to improve my processes and systems to give more real-time information to my customers.

It's not just that he's on top of the function and knows its strengths and weaknesses. Nor that he runs finance like a business, with plenty of references to his customers and their needs. It's how quickly he can explain it in a credible manner. Is your elevator speech in such good shape?

Your respect equity[v]

Of course, none of this works unless you are personally credible. We talked a lot about the various facets that build your credibility as a finance professional in Chapter 2. It's a recipe for success that includes your courage and ethics, your ability to communicate and the working relationships that you build with others. We also heard advice from some seasoned professionals, like Douglas Flint, based on their own experiences. They have been successful in their careers and so their advice carries weight – it has worked for them. And although they are individuals with different backgrounds and experience, working in different industries, the same themes about respect equity emerged through their stories.

Being influential is not about being seen as the expert with the final say. There is too much rough and tumble at the executive level, where your peers are just as smart and opinionated as you are. Map the multiple stakeholders who play alongside you in investment decisions and plan how to engage their buy-in. We mean this quite literally. Identify your key internal stakeholders, understand where and why they sit on a particular topic and plan how you will engage with them to influence them. Sometimes, as we saw in Chapter 2, you will need to exercise indirect influence. Plan who should talk to them on your behalf, rather than you engaging directly with them. You will need to do the same with external stakeholders too, such as creating a relationship with analysts and with your counterpart in an acquisition target. But we suspect that your peers will be your toughest sale.

Bob Gray, the CFO of UBM, puts it pithily: 'If you are determined to do the right thing, there is no tension. My job is to make sure that our stock price isn't hammered and that I don't get fired. The challenge is that sometimes colleagues don't like transparent numbers.' Bob isn't saying that his colleagues don't want to do the right thing. He is endorsing the idea that it isn't just about dishing up the numbers and letting them speak for themselves.

The numbers can expose weaknesses in your colleagues' business areas that might have been blind spots or that are taking time to fix. You need to prepare them before you announce the numbers and you need to be credible for them to accept your numbers.

Courage

You need to have the confidence to say no, even if it is late in the game, if in your view the value proposition is not sufficiently robust. Often the Board is involved in these discussions and so it can be really challenging. If you own the advice you provide, you will garner their trust. This means not holding yourself aloof as the expert, but mucking in with the debate. You have a unique and central role in helping to devise and implement business plans. Don't hold back from making suggestions to the line about broader business changes. It means being part of the business and central to it.

The other place you will need courage is in pushing for change. Investment decisions inevitably involve change and finance can be a key driver for change in the business. That is, you can step forwards and get the ball rolling. This means not being afraid to set and reach for aspirational goals. It means challenging those who continue to dissent, or try to undermine change, once the process has started. And again, it means dealing in an empathic way with people. You will face both rational and irrational responses to change, it's very human. While numbers are your friend in making the business case, they will not support you when you face the anger, fear or excitement that the consequences of following your numbers will arouse. The relationships you have built with others and the trust they have in you will guide you through the messiness of dealing with the aftermath of change. As Bob Gray says, 'The challenge is that sometimes colleagues don't like transparent numbers'. Part of your job is to help your colleagues to accept them nonetheless.

Strategic cost management in finance

We are not intending to provide an exhaustive overview of the literature on how to manage costs. We are going to highlight the four cost management areas that we think are critical. First, understand what you really cost. Then work continuously on getting your costs down. Next think about how, not if, you benchmark your costs against others. Finally, put a value on what you do as a function. Let's turn first to a quick and dirty estimate of what you really cost.

Count noses in the finance factory

Managing your own cost structure is the foundation stone for creating value. It's not just about knowing, 'My direct budget for people who report to me is $21.32 million'. That is just the start. Try to get a handle on how much your finance team costs in total. Make a quick check to confirm the budget reflects fully-loaded costs including accommodation and other internal services, not just salary. This is a far better indicator of how much your firm would spend or save in aggregate by varying your staff levels.

Next, how many of your finance people are embedded in the business lines and how much do they cost? Don't try to get this down to the last penny, resolving internal cost allocations from other functions. Rough estimates will do, so count noses, by salary grade if you can and then multiply out by average salaries and overhead allocations. You want to know if these costs are $10 million, $20 million, or $50 million – not $11.862 million.

Third, what do your service providers cost you? This will probably include a lengthy list of auditors, outsource service providers, banking and M&A advisors (include both retainers and success fees), as well as other consultants. Understand whether these third-party costs are really variable, or whether you would need to add extra internal resources if you dropped these contracts.

If you aren't keeping track of your costs along these lines, start now. Sooner or later these questions are going to be asked, in the context of outsourcing or benchmarking. Be on the front foot in your responses, rather than having to deal with a frustrated CEO, because you will only lose credibility. Once you achieve this kind of cost visibility, you will be able to drive for cost efficiency.

A culture of continuous improvement in costs – beat inflation

Once you know how much you cost, the next step is to see how you can get and keep your costs under control. Ask the kind of questions that establish a culture of continuous cost improvement across finance. What are your trends in costs, year on year? Don't be satisfied with holding costs flat in real terms. No real factory manager would be that passive, in effect it amounts to justifying the status quo. While a good first step would be to absorb inflation, competitive manufacturing organizations target cost reductions of 2–3 per cent beyond that. To make this kind of progress, you need to have a real cost management strategy and a finance leadership team that embraces continuous improvement.

We suggest that you scale your efforts to reflect whether your organization is stagnant, growing, or shrinking, because obviously this has an impact on the demand for your services. Consistent with this trend, make a high-level estimate of what it would take to beat inflation and a bit more. This gives you and your team a target objective. With their input, identify 3–4 access points – not 100 – for achieving these savings. Evaluate the strategic and financial impact of these access points, prioritize your efforts and publicize your progress. This will lead to early successes that can be celebrated among the finance team and leverage value creation opportunities for the whole enterprise.

Adopting strategic cost management makes it easier to create a business case for important investments in finance, such as for ERP[vi] systems and staff training and development. If you continually defer these in order to help meet the organization's annual budget targets, you will be under-investing in your finance business. We all know what that means, we advise against it all the time. It means increasing the risk of exposure and inefficiencies as the years go by. If the business sees you proactively managing finance, it will enhance your credibility in asking for investment in your function.

Selling continuous improvement to finance

Enrolling finance professionals in continuous cost improvement can be challenging. Many of them equate cost reduction with increased risks of reporting errors, missed filing deadlines, too much overtime and deteriorating employee morale. Regrettably, somewhere in their careers they have probably been subject to a slash and burn cost reduction exercise that inflicted all of these ills. At a deeper level, some may fear loss of personal power through reorganization or outsourcing. But if you can create a sense of teamwork and highlight the contribution finance is making to the entire organization, it will work. Encourage your extended finance team to peer review each other's work to help tease out additional opportunities for creating value. This can lead to a self-sustaining virtuous cycle of improvement and value creation–the ultimate investment and return loop. Now let's turn to our third cost management area – benchmarking like you mean it.

Benchmark to find access points for improvement

Have you ever seen a finance colleague abuse, rather than use, benchmarking? Sadly, it's always pretty obvious when they select measures and comparators that only put their organization in a positive light. They are justifying the status quo, rather than looking for real savings. Another example of abuse is completely discounting any value to be gained from benchmarking, claiming that the finance team's circumstances are unique and non-comparable. Neither approach is going to earn you credibility with the executive team.

The main benefit from benchmarking actually comes from the qualitative discussion, not from the quantitative analysis. Benchmark with firms who have tried to make progress in one of these areas you are tackling. Get a general sense of how others approached the problem, the metrics they used to drive their programmes and the results they achieved over time. What sort of challenges did they face? Were they able to sustain the savings, or did the savings erode over time? This is another place where your external network will serve you well. Sometimes you might be offered a general benchmarking survey which will in reality be the platform for a marketing report. This is not what you are looking for. So if you can dive into your network and ask a trusted external advisor to connect you with a few of their other core clients, including some outside your industry, it might raise the bar for all of you.

There is an additional benefit. Once you have a reputation for credible benchmarking skills, you are likely to be invited to help with broader benchmarking across the firm.

Highlight the value of finance

Here is our fourth and final area – how you help others to see the value that finance brings. As we have said before, much of what you do is to play defence through sustaining the control systems and managing for risk. Don't hesitate to demonstrate how this contributes to enterprise value, not least because valuing your defensive activities will help to motivate your finance teams. They are the ones on the barricades who review the creditworthiness of your customers and suppliers, who keep the balance sheet strong and insulated from interest rate and currency fluctuations and who manage engagements with tax authorities and financial regulators. They deserve recognition and encouragement.

But it can be tricky to value the defensive services you provide and to relate this value to its cost. Think about measures such as:

- activity and schedule (progress towards agreed control protocols and embedding agreed risk prevention and mitigation objectives)
- quality (reduction in errors)
- compliance (avoiding fines and penalties).

There are plenty of anecdotes and examples of poor defence tactics that came to light during the 2008 global financial downturn, such as lack of access to credit and reliance on short-term financing. How is your team positioned against these and other failures? Are there strengths you developed during the crisis that can be further leveraged? What did you learn from your customers, suppliers, competitors and other industries, both good and bad?

More specific measures

Let's get more granular about how you can capture the numbers around being really good at defence. We mean going beyond citing the immediate losses that occur from time to time, to show that it's important to keep you around to prevent further losses when things go wrong. We mean being able to articulate the value of finance's contribution to risk management. For example:

- If you have problems in your supply chain, with vendors or customers, can you demonstrate how your finance team limited the loss?
- If the financial markets are volatile, can you determine what was saved, versus the worst case scenario, through your hedging arrangements?
- As you work with regulators and legislators, can you explain how your good working relationships with them limited the extent of fines, penalties, taxes and other changes?
- When crisis hits another firm, can you assess how your risk management tools would be effective against the same challenge and translate this into hypothetical value protected for your firm?

Having a better sense of the value you provide through your defensive activities will help steer the cost management conversation into a more strategic direction. It will also highlight the efforts the finance team undertakes to proactively, rather than reactively, manage value for the firm. Now let's think about your role supporting offensive activities to build the business through investment.

The role of finance in sound investment

Finance is right at the heart of investment. You play multiple roles in investment decisions, such as facilitating strategic planning cycles which provide an overall shape of the business, evaluating specific investment proposals and coordinating the annual budget setting exercise. And yet, despite all this planning, evaluation and budgeting, firms find it hard to grow value. Perhaps it's because these investments aren't so sound after all. As a custodian of value, you need to make sure that, on average and over time across the portfolio of new ideas, your organization comes out a winner. This will be a test of all your skills.

Big ideas or big dreams?

Investment proposals come in many guises – ideas for new facilities, new research, expanding into new markets and purchasing and selling assets and whole companies. Each of these ideas has its own distinct characteristics, but there is an overall theme to all of them. The underpinning theme is the process by which ideas are turned into value. This process is shown in Figure 6.2.

FIGURE 6.2   Process for monitoring investment opportunities

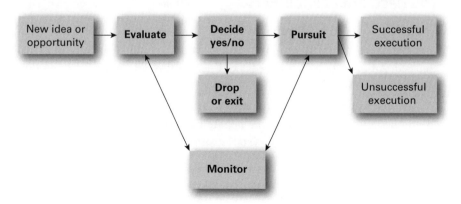

Finance needs to safeguard a disciplined decision-making process and be a counterweight to the project mentality that often fails to consider broader consequences and risks. Thinking about investment like a project tends to drive you in a straight line towards a yes or no answer. We are arguing for a process, rather than a project, mindset. As Figure 6.2 shows, the process starts with identifying new ideas and new opportunities generated from across the organization. Finance should participate in idea generation, to support the evolving conversations and monitor progress as ideas mature. On the other end of the process is execution, where the reality of the investment's potential is actually delivered. In between is the important process loop, highlighted in bold type. Here you are evaluating the idea, deciding whether to move forward or not, pursuing it if you decide to move forward and monitoring the pursuit so that you can re-evaluate whether the initial decision is still valid. Thinking about investment like a process builds in a constant awareness of changes in the environment and keeps your mind open to changing your decision as circumstances evolve.

GIGO[vii]

You probably have established procedures for evaluating opportunities. But it's not enough to make sure the calculations are accurate. Business and project teams tend to have an inherently optimistic bias and finance needs to help them to ground this optimism in reality. Put the input assumptions and outcome probability distributions under a microscope, informed by your organization's own history and experience. Look at external comparators inside and outside your industry and offer guidance that might improve the value proposition. We all want to avoid GIGO, right?

You need broad shoulders

Ultimately, a go/no go decision is required on what gets funded and what gets deferred, dropped or sold. Often these decisions are emotionally charged. An executive may have staked personal reputation on driving this proposal through the system and members of the Board may have become champions. As CFO, your role requires you to steer as well as provide advice, so you need to get involved in the debate but not sucked into the emotion. You need to have the executive relationships, and the confidence, to stand apart and engage with the team to decide what is best in creating value for the firm. You need your respect equity in place.

Once a positive decision has been made, even if you have been overruled, you need to assist in pursuing the opportunity. We will discuss negotiations a bit later, but there are other important areas of support, such as ensuring adequate financing, obtaining required regulatory approval and explaining the opportunity to the investment community. Think proactively about how you and your finance teams can help to ensure the most positive outcome achievable.

During the pursuit, it's easy to get caught up in the action, but you still need to monitor the pursuit, even as you move forwards. As new information arrives, continue to revisit the assumptions that were made in the analysis with the operational team and update models, actions and tactics to adjust to deviations from expectations. Your job is to ensure that finance does as much as possible to achieve a successful pursuit, but also be the voice of reason. In the worst case scenario, you may have to play the sunk cost[viii] card and find a graceful exit strategy, even if colleagues or the media heckle you for pausing or changing course. If you are seen as a partner to the business, your voice will be heard.

Evaluating what you don't fully understand

What if you don't know enough about the investment to be confident in expressing an opinion? Experts are often reluctant to advise outside their own area of expertise and finance is no exception. Let's pause here to look at engineering value management and facility acceptability from operations, to see how we can step outside our knowledge base and still feel comfortable that we are providing sound advice.

Outsiders often assume that operations people always understand the technology that they deal with every day. Here's the secret – they don't. How could anyone be an expert on all the technological minutiae in modern process technologies? But this doesn't mean that you either leave investment decisions to the experts or simply go with their advice. You ask a series of straightforward structured questions that help you to understand the implications of investment options on the business as a whole. These questions clarify why an operation's investment can give strategic advantage and how managers can make such investments work in practice.

Here's how we can apply this to finance. You also will need to assess investment opportunities that are outside your area of expertise. There are three generic classes of evaluation criteria that can help you:

1 The *feasibility* of the investment, that is, the degree of difficulty in adopting it, and the investment of time, effort and money that will be needed.

2 The *acceptability* of the investment, that is, how much it moves the business towards its strategic objectives while achieving or exceeding financial returns.

3 The *vulnerability* associated with the investment, that is, the extent to which the firm is exposed if things go wrong and the risk that is run by choosing the investment.

We'll look at each of them in turn.

Drilling down on feasibility

All investment decisions need a variety of resources if they are to be implemented successfully – financial, technical and so on. If the resources required to implement an investment are greater than those that are either available or can be obtained, the investment is not feasible. How can we find out if the various types of resource that the investment might need match up to what is available? Three broad questions can help us here:

1 Which technical or human skills are required to implement the investment? Every investment will need a set of skills so that it can be successfully implemented. You need to see if you have or can acquire the skills you identify, especially if the investment is completely novel.

2 What quantity of resources is required to implement the investment? Determining the quantity of resources, such as people, facilities, space, time and so on, required to implement the investment is important because it is time dependent. For example, a lack of sufficient process engineers might not rule out a particular investment, but it could restrict when it is adopted.

3 Can the operation cope with the degree of change in resource requirements? Even if the necessary resources can be obtained by the organization, the degree of change in the total resource position might be infeasible. If the rate of change in resource requirements is too dramatic, it might make the investment infeasible.

Now let's turn to acceptability

Finance professionals are used to evaluating the acceptability of an investment in financial terms. But two further categories of evaluation are sometimes neglected. These are the investment's impact on process performance and its resource characteristics. We are trying to get a broader picture of how the investment will improve our quality, customer service and capture scarce resources for us. Here are some more questions that can be helpful.

Questions relevant to process performance are:

- What impact will the investment have on quality? Does it provide something better or different that customers value, or reduce variability and so contribute to conformance quality?
- How does the investment affect speed? Does it enable a faster response to customers, or speed the throughput of internal processes?
- How does the investment affect dependability? Does it enable products and/or services to be delivered more dependably, or enhance the dependability of processes within the operation?
- How does the investment affect flexibility? Does it allow the operation to be more responsive to changes in customer demand?

For resource characteristics, we are trying to build up a picture of the contribution that the investment can make to building capabilities and endowing us with sustainable competitive advantage:

- Does the investment capture scarce resources, denying them to competitors?
- Does the investment capture resources that are difficult to move out of the business?
- Does the investment capture resources that are difficult to copy, for example because of patent protection?
- Does the investment capture resources for which it is difficult to create a substitute?

And finally, vulnerability

By this we mean risk and we have already devoted considerable space to this topic. For example, specific skills may be needed if the investment is to be installed, maintained, upgraded and controlled effectively. Are they present or available? Run the riskometer over the deal as we laid out in Chapter 5.

It doesn't quite end here. We have looked at taking the decision to invest and also how we should consider our ability to execute effectively as part of the decision-making process. But we also need to have the right set of options available for the future. We turn to this next.

Understanding option value

Finance can help to provide a competitive edge by understanding the option value of your firm's opportunities. Do you think in terms of fixed outcomes, or an evolving array of possibilities? Do you think about clearly defined project steps, or a sequence of stepping stones that reveal themselves only as you move from stone to stone? We agree that you need to be able to drive towards target outcomes. But you need to develop the capability to think in terms of option value as well.

Options come in a variety of shapes and sizes. They include the flexibility to change your mind, the opportunity to expand from a base level of activity, the chance to test a new technology or market with a low level of risk and the possibility of shifting risk consequences to others. Your investment opportunities will present varying ranges of options and thinking in terms of option value may cause you to re-prioritize your firm's capital investment programme. If the options currently in the investment portfolio don't match your strategic intent, you will need to rebalance. Options are rarely free, so make sure they are worth paying for and certainly take any free ones that are offered.

Assessing the value and cost of options is partly intellectual, partly based on experience and partly intuitive. It makes sense to record and discuss your experience with options to build your capability in this area. You can bet that some of your best competitors and counterparties are focused on doing just that.

Execution

The contracts have just been signed, the empty champagne bottles have all been cleared away and you are now the proud owner of a new opportunity. We are now in the execution box from Figure 6.2. But you will have noticed that there were two boxes – one successful and the other, unsuccessful. No value is created when the ink is dry, only the potential to create value. Value is delivered after the signing date, by imposing and reacting to changes in your existing business. And so, you and your finance team still have a big responsibility post-closing – to manage the risk of change. How do you make sure that expected value moves from the spreadsheet to the bottom line?

Managing the risk of change

What exactly is this? Let's take an example. There's a North African natural gas processing facility that was initially built as an open air facility. After a few years, a sun-cover was installed to give the workers a bit of shade. A decade later, a new computer system was installed and walls and insulation were added along with air conditioning. It all seemed so sensible, until the whole thing blew up one afternoon – as minute quantities of gas accumulated over time in the now enclosed facility. That's what we mean by management of change risk.

It is one thing to support your existing businesses and quite another to identify the myriad of things that you don't understand fully about your new opportunity. This is not the time to walk away, because you can add further value. While each opportunity will have its own detailed considerations, you should consider creating an execution office in each case, to insert financial experts who understand the transaction, who know the contract by heart and who can look under every rock and close out exposures quickly.

Here are some of the activities your execution office should cover:

- Monitor cash flow and make sure that working capital doesn't suddenly disappear or that spending doesn't get ahead of government approvals.
- Track operational performance and help intervene if milestones are not achieved – on staffing, ordering long lead-time items, installing new systems and securing land.
- Help defend your rights, because others may try to marginalize your position while you are getting established.

The first year is particularly critical. As your execution team completes its work, there is one last management of change step: to ensure a seamless handoff to the finance team that will manage this opportunity on an ongoing basis. If these post-closing issues are given proper attention and sustained follow-through, your efforts will help cement finance's reputation as a solid contributor to the value of the firm.

Were you involved in the negotiations themselves, as the deal took shape? Another way you create value is in your skills as a negotiator and we look at these skills in the final section of the chapter.

Finance and business negotiations

We mean here negotiations in its most generic sense, covering transactions such as acquisitions, divestments and mergers, but also contracts, marketing arrangements, research agreements and joint ventures. Defined in this way, negotiations involve the process of scouting out new ideas, partners and potential deals and also cover the process of agreeing terms and recording the transaction in written and legally binding contracts.

Most of you will have had at least peripheral exposure to negotiations, but have you had direct experience? Suddenly, you are expected to play a critical leadership role at the executive table. We are not going to provide detailed techniques on prospecting for business or across-the-table negotiations.[ix] But for those of you who are deal novices or simply need a refresher to stay focused, we offer here a checklist of eight important themes.

1 Know the *value proposition* of the proposed transaction and the validity of the assumptions supporting this assessment. Don't be distracted by the headline price. Make sure the entire business model of the deal fits together – how goods and services come together to create value and how risks and liabilities are apportioned. The CFO has a major role to play at the tactical level, through ensuring a good screening process, so that each element of the transaction is properly evaluated and risks are mitigated.

2 Identify your *walk-away position* – your negotiating limits and your boundary conditions in terms of return and resource commitment. You'll often be asked for 'just a little bit more'. There are cultural characteristics too – negotiating with Russians is very different from negotiating with Indians. Don't get caught up in deal fever, which will be worse if big closing bonuses are at stake. Recognize that you don't have to close every deal and that walking away feeling disappointed is far better than signing up to a loser. So you will want a robust process in place as you debate with line executives any recommendations to relax your boundary conditions.

3 Make sure you *understand the transaction dependencies* that are required to close a deal. Is your business plan realistic and have you mapped out in detail all the pieces that have to fit together to make this a workable and value-creating part of your enterprise?

For example, if you are trying to create a new overseas joint venture with a host government that is subject to the government's power of approval or veto, do you understand how the government might be able to block progress in the name of national security?

4 In mergers or joint ventures, make sure you have *strategic and tactical alignment with your counterparty*. Understand what each party brings to the table, what each wants from the transaction and confirm that you are not 'sleeping in the same bed but dreaming different dreams'. It can be very helpful to create a pro-forma business plan, also known as the negotiating case, to give both sides a vehicle for airing different and potentially misaligned points of view. Create multiple points of access inside your counterparty, to understand their priorities, their decision-making process and their tolerance for creative approaches. Expect them to try to create option value for themselves, especially if you hear the phrase 'these really are just trivialities not worth troubling ourselves over'. Sometimes, granting an option you are willing to concede becomes the key that closes the deal.

5 *Understand the competitive process and your competitors.* Be clear whether you are participating in a transparent bidding process, or parallel bilateral negotiations.[x] It is notoriously hard to create value in a transparent bidding situation with more than about three or four bidders, as you are always exposed to 'the marginal idiot'. This is the rude description of the bidder who doesn't quite get it and submits much too high a bid in the sealed envelope (it might even be you). Parallel bilateral negotiations are also tough. It is hard to separate how much the purchaser is bluffing, in order to extract maximum value from you, from genuine feedback on what you actually need to do to emerge as the winner. To prepare for the pressure and postured threats, you need to understand fully your competition. What can they offer that you can't and vice versa? For example, a state enterprise might bring intergovernmental benefits, while you might be able to offer access to markets or technologies.

6 Keep track of the *chase costs*. Know how much you are prepared to commit to a potentially losing effort. Significant value can be lost chasing deals for long periods of time. It's a bit like sitting in a stationary taxicab with the meter running. Sometimes these projects are pursued within large units, where the chase costs are dwarfed by base business expenditure. Modest amounts of annual funding, spent

over a period of many years, can result in an unwelcome write-off if the deal fails or a big sunk cost burden if the deal succeeds.

7 Also *watch the clock*. Deals usually have a natural but unwritten rhythm. Experienced negotiators know when they are at the 'now or never' point – when their counterparty really will walk away from their last offer. And smart negotiators will watch for seemingly unrelated events that can also help you to manage the clock to your benefit. Does your counterparty have a hidden deadline, possibly related to local politics, which is either driving the importance of this deal, or alternatively, which reduces the perceived value of the deal once the deadline is missed? There was one deal in the Middle East which was initialled and only awaited signature by the head of state. But the head of state died and when his successor wasn't interested in the deal, there was nothing left to do but close up shop and write off the chase costs. (A fun though true story, but obviously an extreme case.)

8 Lastly, you need to *protect the enterprise's reputation*. Occasionally business development teams will execute non-binding memoranda of understanding, to help secure their position against the competition. You need to ensure this is done in a disciplined fashion, because lasting reputation damage can result from a press release and a big public event that imply commitment before the underlying commercial analysis has been completed. Once the deal is done, be cautious about selling it on to someone else, because your counterparty, or the approving government, may become unnecessarily annoyed if they conclude that they left too much money on the table. And most important of all, as we said above, stay with the deal through execution, to make sure your new business performs as expected by all stakeholders. This builds lasting reputation and the potential for the next deal.

These eight themes are just handrails to get you started and to build your awareness and confidence as quickly as possible. Experience is the best teacher. And don't forget to train your extended finance team in these skills as well. One good way is to let them join negotiations led by experts. In fact, the role of observer is one of the more important ones at the negotiating table. The finance professional can watch for body language, take detailed notes, and see how well your deal team executes against their pre-agreed tactics.

Summary ... and looking ahead

This chapter was again focused on your role as a custodian of value. Allister Wilson, the partner at Ernst & Young who helped us in Chapter 5 to debunk the flocks of black swans being claimed when things go wrong, is typically robust in his view:

> There has to be one version of the truth in your financial numbers. You can't have different numbers being used to communicate internally compared with externally. The market cannot lose confidence in the integrity and rigour of your numbers. It must believe in what it is getting.

Being a CFO today is exciting and challenging. You are essentially running a business within a business. As line executives see you applying business principles to the finance function, their confidence in you as a business partner will grow. Your credibility in arguing for value creation will be enhanced as they see that you don't just talk about it, but also apply the same principles to finance. You need to be an active player in value creation for the enterprise, because you have a lot to offer. Not only will you and your team contribute significantly to the value of the enterprise, you will create the foundation for a lasting legacy when you hand the baton to your successor.

Chapter 7 – self-assessment

In the final chapter we offer some concluding thoughts. But our most valuable contribution is the self-assessment exercise that we encourage you to take. There are two versions. The first is a list of open questions that will help you to think through generally the CFO attributes that we have set out in this book. The second version is shorter with a scale to self-assess how you score today. Knowing how you score today will give you an understanding of what you need to do next to keep developing. Whether you are just starting out on a career in finance, or whether your next role is likely to be as CFO, or whether you are an experienced CFO – we know that you will find food for thought in this self-assessment. It will help you to take the next step.

Notes

i *From CFO to CEO: Route to the top*, by Tibor Gedeon, Karel Pobuda, Andrzej Maciejewski and Robert Nowakowski, SpencerStuart December 2009, ibid Chapter 1.

ⁱⁱ IRR = Internal Rate of Return, NPV = Net Present Value.

ⁱⁱⁱ For those of you who are not Harry Potter fans, dementor is the name
J.K. Rowling gives to black spirits who suck the life out of others, feeding on
their happiness and destroying it. This is a bit extreme. We are just suggesting
that you might also want to pour cold water on investment ideas from time
to time.

ⁱᵛ This is a simplified variant of the famous BCG-matrix. The Boston Consulting
Group analysis portfolio diagram is a chart that was created by Bruce
Henderson for the Boston Consulting Group in 1968 to help corporations
analyse their business units or product lines and allocate resources. A user-
friendly alternative would be Malcolm McDonald's matrix, derived from GE
McKinsey and BCG, *Marketing Plans: How to Prepare Them, How to Use
Them*, 7th edition, by Malcolm McDonald and Hugh Wilson, John Wiley,
2011.

ᵛ This is how Mohit Bhatia, CFO of Genpact, describes CFO credibility.

ᵛⁱ Enterprise resource planning (ERP) integrates internal and external management
information across an entire organization. ERP systems automate this
activity with an integrated software application. Its purpose is to facilitate
the flow of information between all business functions inside the boundaries
of the organization and manage the connections to outside stakeholders.
Chapter 4 ibid.

ᵛⁱⁱ Garbage in, garbage out. The numbers you conclude are only as strong as the
accuracy and assumptions on which they are based.

ᵛⁱⁱⁱ If you work in finance, you will know this expression. If not, it means don't try
to hold on to the money you have already invested by pursuing a poor option.
Wave goodbye to the original investment, because if the option is poor, you will
only continue to lose money.

ⁱˣ Two excellent texts you could consult here are the classic *Getting to Yes*, by
Roger Fisher and William Ury, too many editions and versions to list here;
and *You Can Negotiate Anything*, by Herb Cohen; Lyle Stuart, 1980 and
multiple editions since, as well as being a New York Times best-seller.

ˣ Transparent bidding = every company submits their sealed bid and you only
get one chance to decide how much to bid. At the given time, the sealed bids
are opened in a public setting (hence transparent) and the winner is the highest
bidder. Parallel bilateral negotiations give full discretion to the vendor to decide
how they want to value potentially differently structured bids and decide who
should get the award.

A custodian of value

> *The CFO's top priority is to understand how value is created and destroyed. The global financial services' crisis happened because the leaders of the banks lost sight of how value is created. They thought they were creating value in their activities and all they were doing was moving risk around.*
>
> **ALLISTER WILSON,[i] PARTNER, ERNST & YOUNG**

Is the bar too high?

All that said, as you read this book, did you sometimes think that we were setting the bar too high? That this paragon CFO could not possibly exist? Some do – and we have interviewed them for this book. But how achievable is it?

Patrick Pichette, Google's CFO,[ii] thinks it is achievable throughout finance:

> Google continues to attract and retain immensely high-caliber talent. In consequence of that, their expectation is that they're going to have a job that is immensely interesting. We naturally attract people who want their financial forecasts to work – and they're going to work like mad to make sure that this only takes one day of their week. Then they're going to spend the other four days of the week reinventing the business, doing crazy analyses that are going to be deeply fact based, in order to find key insights.

Isn't that interesting? A whole finance function that sees running the numbers as something they need to get out of the way so that they can spend the majority of their time on future value creation. Oh, and this is the company that can close its books in three days too. They also have a dedicated M&A team and grow through acquisitions, so they have their fair share of legacy systems to cope with. Their reality is not that remote from yours.

Bernard Katompa, the CEO of Liberty Africa, had expectations of himself when he was CFO and holds the same expectations of his CFO today: 'The CFO must have a helicopter view of the business. Avoid being a number cruncher. Instead, be the traffic manager and understand the numbers and what makes them. Understand the business as a whole to help those who operate it to be more efficient.'

Bob Gray, CFO of UBM, agrees. Remember, he told us in Chapter 1, 'My role as a CFO is to push the business on the numbers to get to the value drivers.' How close are you to the value-driven, helicopter CFO? Here is the first version of the self-assessment tool that we hope will prompt you to ask yourself some searching questions.

Self-assessment

Chapter 1: Becoming a custodian of value

Look at your calendar – how are you spending your time? How much is going into tactical firefighting? How much time are you spending on penetrating the various aspects of finance, to determine how better to protect and create value? How much time is spent attending meetings and compare this with how much time you are spending forging relationships? How much time are you spending externally – learning and sharing with peers?

Take a look at your own background – and measure this against the spectrum of finance job families presented in the Appendix.[iii] Which are the functions where you cut your teeth? Is there anything new to learn from the current generation of incumbents? Which are the functions where you have no practical experience, no dirt under your fingernails? How confident are you of your abilities to ask penetrating questions in these areas, to make sure you are not overlooking major areas of risk because you don't want to look unschooled? If you do have knowledge gaps, how are you closing them?

How comfortable are you commenting on and intervening in business areas outside of finance? To what extent do others come to you to help work through thorny and unwieldy problems besetting the organization?

Take a look at your direct reports. Are they highly competent subject matter experts within a narrow field of expertise, or are they developing breadth and curiosity in other fields? To what extent have they been able to achieve meaningful development positions outside of finance, especially leadership roles in other functional areas and in line businesses? Where you see any gaps, what are you doing about it?

What are you doing to develop the next generation of finance leaders? Are you content to let them work within their functional silos, or do you have an active development programme that manages the tension between creating both deep functional expertise and broad awareness of the essence of other functional areas? How actively are you promoting teamwork across finance – do you just mouth the words, or do you take an active leadership role?

Chapter 2: Strategic leadership

How do you show up as a leader? To what extent are you an examplar of executive leadership and to what extent are you giving ground to others simply because they are more aggressive? Are you able to role model characteristics that engender the trust and respect of others, rather than their grudging compliance? To what extent are you an advocate for your people, or do they sense that you will throw them under a bus if you need to get out of a problem? How high is your respect equity across the business? How influential are you? Do people trust your personal integrity and the integrity of the numbers you produce?

How about your communication skills? Are you solely focused on the numbers and your written text, or are you able to tell a compelling story that helps people understand the deeper impact of your message? Have you had training in presentation and listening skills and if not, why not? When you have a difficult message, to what extent do you pull your punches so as not to upset others – and confuse everyone in the process?

Consider three specific dilemmas that you face in trying to be a strategic partner to the business, at the same time as maintaining the independence required as a CFO. What makes them dilemmas and what are you doing to balance the tension? Which one is giving you the most heartburn (be honest with yourself, the odds are that your toughest dilemmas have little to do with the specifics of finance and more to do with interpersonal engagement)? If none of your dilemmas seems very challenging, you probably aren't trying hard enough to be a leader.

How healthy are your networks? How much time do you spend cultivating your networks? Are your relationships fairly superficial or deeply trusting, where you can honestly share problems and concerns? Are you just networking with like-minded people in your own industry, or do you have relationships that challenge you? If your networks are underdeveloped, what are you doing to address this?

Do you know your potential derailers? When is the last time you got constructive feedback that actually meant anything and that gave you leverage points for action? Do you know how to keep your strengths under control and how to keep from annoying others by overplaying your hand? Are you aware of instances when the body language or lack of verbal support from others has indicated that you missed your mark? If none of this makes any sense to you, have you considered how to get expert help to make visible this important blind spot?

Chapter 3: The finance factory

Think about how much real experience you have with process mapping and management. Can you distinguish what is required to map out a process – as opposed to a Gantt chart that is used to map out a project? Think about how you talk about processes in your firm – is it patronizing support for 'silent running', or is it clear understanding and commitment to the essentials of your business?

To what extent are you aware of the key one or two core processes in each of your major functional areas of finance? How do the leaders in each of these functional areas talk about their processes? What do they have in place to monitor and improve their processes? How do you recognize and reward them for this work?

Have you spent any significant time with your (or someone else's) outsource service provider? Have you asked them to show you how they manage high-volume, low-variety processes? What have you learned from what disrupts these processes, how they work to manage the disruptions and how they improve the processes? What can they teach you about how to motivate staff in this area?

Take one of your areas where the process is low-volume, high-variety. Working with your leaders in this area, can you get the objectives and desired outcomes straight, decide how much value adding you want to do and what resources are required to really manage this process properly, prior to actually running and monitoring the process? Can you invoke the discipline to set quarterly targets to improve this process on a sustained basis?

Ask each of your functional leaders to identify a process that is causing them problems. Can they plot their process on the product–process spectrum and identify which processes are too rigid or too flexible for requirements? Can they work together to define how the process flow needs to be adjusted, whether more or less use of automation is required and whether the jobs involved are properly defined?

Chapter 4: Establishing and maintaining robust controls

What is your attitude to control? Do you have deep knowledge and expertise in manipulating the inputs to a system to obtain the desired effect on the outputs – or do you see control as something that either is fairly pedestrian, or else constrains the creativity required to be successful in business? To what extent are you communicating these very personal attitudes subconsciously to other executives and to your finance organization? Can you do more than say 'control is important' – can you be a believable champion for this important role of the CFO?

How much personal time have you actually spent at the base of the control pyramid – understanding internal controls and systems and processes? Are you able to articulate to your own leadership team how weaknesses in these areas undermine the integrity of operational analysis, business reporting and strategic planning? To what extent are the professionals in internal control and systems and processes treated on a par with your strategic planners – in terms of management attention and recognition?

To what extent are you leading your executive team to be champions of control across the firm? Are they role models of integrity – or do they say the words but have 'special approaches' when they themselves are involved? To what extent have you exposed them to the external risks – such as money laundering or terrorist financing – that can come from lapses in basic control?

Can you take a simple control process – one either from your business or from your finance organization – and plot the inputs, the operation and the outputs – as well as the monitoring systems and the intervention points? How well situated are you to move from the desktop to the real world and monitor and intervene in the process as it operates day to day? To what extent do you spend a significant portion of your own time personally attending to the design and monitoring of your key processes?

Can you take the skills you have developed in process management and use them in activities where the objectives are ambiguous, or where the outputs aren't measurable? How confident are you in your abilities to exercise judgement or political control?

Chapter 5: Deepening and spreading risk management

Can you identify the inherent risks in your control processes as they fatigue over time? What have you done about the more significant of these risks – do you have preventive mechanisms in place to reduce their probability, as well as mitigation plans to reduce their impact?

Have you evaluated the nature of the processes by which your firm identifies and assesses risk? Is it purely bottom up, or just top down, or more holistic? Does it incorporate learning from risk events that have occurred external to the firm and even external to your industry? How capable are you of identifying low-probability, high-impact risks?

How deeply have you examined the presuppositions that underpin your approach to the management of risk? Do you actively consider how your layers of protection might fail you and how your mitigation plans might not be available as expected when called upon?

How confident are you in moving beyond the management of financial risks into the realm of business risk? Are you able to translate your intuitive concerns into penetrating questions that get to the heart of the risk exposures? And are you able to sustain the debate with business champions who are more familiar with the details – and perhaps with more overall seniority – but who are less cognizant of the risks?

Are the risk prevention and mitigation plans cascaded to the appropriate levels of your organization and do you have an active process for monitoring the effectiveness of these activities? How embedded are your processes for risk recovery and learning – so that your organization continuously builds risk management capability over time?

Chapter 6: Growing value through investment

Do you have an honest assessment of whether you are seen as a true partner of the business, or have you and your finance team settled for lesser roles such as umpire or cheerleader? Since this question gets to the heart of many of the dualities you need to manage, can you – and the business – articulate specific examples of where value is being protected and created by this partnership? And can you actually quantify this value in rough terms?

Do you have a strategy for managing costs and investments across finance, or are you alternatively relying on generous budgets or being a victim of mindless cost reduction? Do you have a firm handle on your costs and do you examine how you might vary the cost/service relationship by changing your portfolio of services? In a cost constrained world, are you able to find ways to beat inflation and best in class benchmarks – if not overall, then in some of your major cost areas?

Can you go beyond the numbers and look closely at investment projects championed by others to see whether the organization has the capability to make them feasible? Can you determine whether projects truly advance your strategy and can you explain the implications and risks if the investment goes wrong? Can you help the organization to understand if there is real option value in the proposal?

How active are you in the really big investment decisions – do you act like a true internal board member, or are you more focused on calculations and compliance? Have you developed the ability to simultaneously pursue an investment target and also stand back to make sure the target is worth pursuing? And can you lead your finance organization to making sure the value of the investment is really delivered once the project or deal is launched?

Have you developed a savvy marketing approach for your finance team, or are you quietly hoping that others will see the value for themselves? To what extent have you determined the three to four things that really matter to your fellow executives when it comes to the contribution from finance? And have you found an effective way of presenting the facts, so that they are enthusiastically affirmed by the executives, rather than politely tolerated and then dismissed?

Twenty questions

We really encourage you to work with the more conversational discourse above, both because it is intentionally provocative and also because it adds a little more context to each of the questions it poses.

For those of you who like numbers, here is the shorter, self-scoring version. When you have completed it for yourself, complete it for one of your most talented staff members. That is, we are not only interested in how competent you are at the expanded CFO role, but also in how well you are developing your people to be as good as you. Any score below 3 requires immediate attention.

Score yourself from 1 (low) to 5 (high) on the following questions:

1 Can you keep to a minimum the time you spend firefighting to keep up with the basics of your job?   `1  2  3  4  5`

2 How well do you cover the spectrum of finance responsibilities set out in the Appendix?   `1  2  3  4  5`

3 How strong is your respect equity inside and outside finance?   `1  2  3  4  5`

4 Are you a great communicator (without PowerPoint)?   `1  2  3  4  5`

5 Can you name the top three dilemmas you are juggling?   `1  2  3  4  5`

6 Do you know your derailers?   `1  2  3  4  5`

7 Do you know your top three processes in finance?   `1  2  3  4  5`

8 Can you map these processes?   `1  2  3  4  5`

9 Can you plot your core processes on the volume–variety spectrum?   `1  2  3  4  5`

10 Can you identify which processes are too rigid or too flexible for requirements and make the necessary adjustments?   `1  2  3  4  5`

11 How well do you understand your control systems and processes? | 1 2 3 4 5 |

12 Do you understand the wide range of controls you need to manage, from the fundamental to the strategic? | 1 2 3 4 5 |

13 Can you articulate the value you create through strong controls? | 1 2 3 4 5 |

14 Do you have a bottom-up and top-down process for identifying the key risks in your business? | 1 2 3 4 5 |

15 How well do you learn from risk events inside and outside your business? | 1 2 3 4 5 |

16 Can you manage business risk (as well as financial risk)? | 1 2 3 4 5 |

17 Do you run finance like a business? | 1 2 3 4 5 |

18 Do you sit alongside your business executives and have an equal voice in which investments your organization should undertake? | 1 2 3 4 5 |

19 How well networked are you, outside your business and industry? | 1 2 3 4 5 |

20 How well are you developing the next generation of finance leaders? | 1 2 3 4 5 |

Conclusion

Our fundamental belief is that your training and intellect deserve a more rewarding career than scrambling to keep up with the ever-increasing demands of the business for management information. We invite you to swap your current job of keeping multiple plates spinning on the ends of wobbly sticks for the job of strategic business advisor.

We'd like the last word to come from a CFO. In Chapter 2, we talked about the importance of integrity. It has always been important for leaders. It has never been more important for finance leaders. If we can't trust the people who keep the scores for us, there is no strong foundation for our future.

We wish you the very best of luck.

Bob Gray, CFO of UBM: 'At the very heart, our job must be based on our principles. It comes down to is it right or wrong – not whether it's IFRS 3 compliant.'

Notes

[i] Allister and others recommended a book to us – a more classic finance book on value (Return on Capital, stock market, growth and so on). If Allister likes it, it's worth mentioning. *The Four Cornerstones of Corporate Finance*, by Tim Koller, Richard Dobbs and Bill Huyett, McKinsey & Co. Inc., November 2010.

[ii] *McKinsey Quarterly* August 2011, an interview by James Manyika.

[iii] There are many books and articles that provide a ground level assessment of the more technical aspects of your job. You know where to find them. Helpful websites are the Public Company Accounting Oversight Board (pcaobus.org); the Securities and Exchange Commission (sec.gov); the Financial Services Authority (fsa.gov.uk). Three detailed briefs from them that could help are: **http://pcaobus.org/Standards/Auditing/Pages/Auditing_Standard_5.aspx**; **http://www.sec.gov/rules/interp/2007/33-8810.pdf**; **http://www.fsa.gov.uk/pubs/policy/bnr_firm-framework.pdf**

APPENDIX
The finance spectrum

In Chapter 1 we described the breadth of finance responsibilities that are held by the CFO. We described this broad set of responsibilities as the finance spectrum.

Here we attempt a comprehensive overview[i] of the job content of the spectrum. It is a list of the activities for which the CFO is responsible or in which the CFO is involved. Where the CFO is responsible, these work streams report to the CFO. Where the CFO is involved, it is because the individuals doing the work typically come from the finance function and often return to the finance function as they progress in their careers.

Not every organization is set up like this and no doubt your finance function will have a slightly different list. We are making the simple point that this is a pretty impressive job scope. It illustrates the wide breadth of responsibilities for the twenty-first-century CFO.

Financial accounting, control and reporting

- Outsourced services management
- Shared services management
- Accounting systems (IT) management
- General ledger accounting
- Consolidation accounting
- System of internal control and regime for financial regulatory compliance
- Delegation of authority management
- Accounting policy
- Preparation of external financial statements and statutory filings
- Auditor meetings and explanations
- Financial regulatory compliance

Management accounting and reporting

- Cost control accounting
- Project management accounting
- Performance unit reporting and analysis
- Line of business reporting and analysis
- Division reporting and analysis
- Enterprise-level reporting and analysis
- Forecasting

Internal audit

- Preparation and monitoring of enterprise risk management processes
- Evaluation of internal controls at asset and enterprise levels

Treasury

- Financial frame for the enterprise
- Sources and uses of cash plan
- Long- and short-term debt portfolio management – enterprise and joint venture
- Project and structured financing
- Equity management – buy-back and new issuance
- Cash management – collections, payables, short-term investment
- Banking relations
- Credit analysis
- Pension and 401k management
- Insurance and alternative risk transfer management
- Real estate management
- Currency management
- Leasing

Risk

- Coordination and direction for risk committees
- Financial risk management processes and content judgement
- Articulation of shareholders' perspective of risk for the executive

- Authority and boundary designation for enterprise risk officers
- Integrity of market, credit, operational and financial risk tools and instruments

Investor/media relations

- Explanation of quarterly and annual results
- Engagement with major investors
- Annual report preparation
- Analyst meetings
- Trade, industry and other public presentations
- Government meetings and advocacy

Tax

- Tax accounting
- Tax reporting
- Tax planning and optimization of post-tax outcomes
- Tax advocacy and dispute resolution

Investment analysis

- Project evaluation
- Line of business evaluation
- Allocation of capital

Strategic planning

- Competitor analysis
- Customer analysis
- Product/service analysis
- Portfolio analysis
- Scenario analysis
- Presentations/communications with Board of Directors, investors and financial press

Deal making

- New business development
- Evaluation of financing and tax options

- Negotiations for acquisitions, joint ventures, alliances, divestments, etc.
- Management of change post-transaction

Mergers, acquisitions and divestments

- Target analysis and evaluation
- Integration/separation

Coordination and integration

- Cooperation between the financial functions (Finance, Tax, Treasury, Audit, M&A)
- Deployment and development of the resource of technical financial people

Note

[i] We are grateful to Andrew Grant, who leads the Finance University at BP, for support in compiling this list.

INDEX